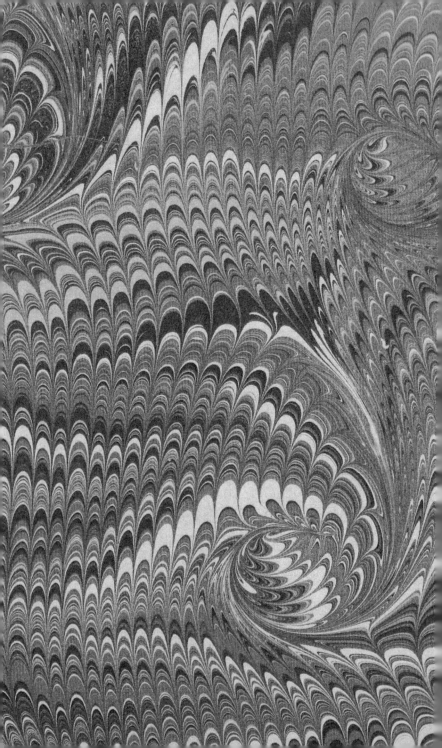

HONK, CONK
and
SQUACKET

Fabulous and Forgotten Sound-words
from a Vanished Age of Listening

Compiled by
I. M. RAWES

THE LONDON SOUND SURVEY

Published by the London Sound Survey
www.soundsurvey.org.uk

A CIP catalogue record for this book
is available from the British Library

ISBN 978-1-5272-0160-6

Typesetting and design by I. M. Rawes
Printed by Imprint Academic Ltd, Exeter

Stephen jerked his thumb towards the window, saying:
—That is God.
Hooray! Ay! Whrrwhee!
—What? Mr Deasy asked.
—A shout in the street, Stephen answered, shrugging his shoulders.

James Joyce, Ulysses

INTRODUCTION

This is a book of old sound-related words I've compiled from sources including out-of-copyright encyclopedias, slang dictionaries, textbooks, patents, and more. A good many were found in the English dialect surveys of the late 19th century, for which local words for things were collected county by county.

They range from morsels lifted from the pungent stew of Middle English to the slangs of the early 20th century. There are examples from the former colonies where English was introduced, often supplanting local languages but sometimes exchanging words with them, or creating hybrids to add to the lexicons of pidgin and creole speech.

In this book you can discover the meanings of mysterious words like *cockathodon*, *wagga-pot*, *skerry-kabberish* and *snirt*. You'll also find some new ways to describe irritating habits and dispositions, such as *bladder-mouth*, *mum-chance* and *squalloch*. Or you might be especially intrigued by a particular place, and to help satisfy this a gazetteer at the back lists the words by county and country.

But, above all, I hope to share with you the same immersive sense of past ways of life which crept up on me as I did my research. Sound is a good way to engage the imagination and thinking about old sounds, and how people might have listened to them, seemed to make a vanished world press a little closer to the other side of the veil.

Recorded sound fulfills this purpose excellently, but it's not been around much longer than the oldest people alive today. Whilst early photographs were capturing detailed street scenes in the 1830s, the first location sound recordings in Britain were not made until 1888. In that year, the Handel Festival was held at the Crystal Palace in south London, and it featured a 4,000-strong choir. One of Thomas Edison's representatives recognised this as a sufficiently loud sound-source to etch onto the rotating wax cylinders of the newly-invented phonograph, and so the Festival was recorded. The cylinders have survived to the present and on them the voices of the choir are faint and ineffably sweet as they rise above and fall beneath storms of surface noise. It is the sound of time.

Very few recordings of street life and daily activities can still be found from between then and the 1930s. The BBC had produced some outside broadcasts in the 1920s but either didn't record them or else its recordings were dumped during the 1932 move from the old studios in Savoy Hill to Broadcasting House. In 1933, someone thought to load a microphone together with a cumbersome amplifier and disc-cutting machines on board a motor launch for *Night on London's River*. The broadcast took the form of a tour along part of the Thames complete with a languid running commentary. Sound travels well across water and ships' hooters and dockers' cries can be heard quite clearly.

By 1935 the BBC had purchased their own recording vehicles, at first using modified laundry vans, and enthusiastic young broadcasters began to explore all kinds of places. They made recordings in dockyards and schoolrooms, in auction houses and fairgrounds. They captured the voices of soapbox orators and their hecklers, the urgent patter of market traders and the singing games of schoolchildren. In total, perhaps two hundred such recordings of ordinary British life, most of them only a minute or so long, survive from the pre-war period.

They summon up a vigorous and eccentric world which might have seemed more familiar to the Victorian compilers of the dialect surveys than to us. For centuries, urban sound-words had been drawn mostly from the life of the streets, with its cast of beggars, musicians, and itinerant traders: *bawlers*, *bottlers*, *patterers*, *yowpers*, *blind-harpers*, *maunders* and *weepers*. Others came from an old substrate of thieves' slang, partly shared with Parleyaree, the language of fairgrounds and showmen. From there it found its way into the gay slang of Polari, which showed some of its pedigree through terms like *hearing-cheat*, an echo of the *cackling-chete* and *quacking-chete* of the 17th century.

Books and pamphlets from the 18th and early 19th centuries promised to reveal the secrets of street slang in a racy, scurrilous way. Whatever specialised vocabularies had been devised by the urban artisanal classes went largely unremarked. Perhaps the lives of craftsmen were considered less entertainingly Hobbesian, or else their ranks, better organised than those of poorer citizens, were more difficult to infiltrate and report back on. It may even have been that they had fewer words of interest, but this seems unlikely given the variety of trades and workplaces and the numbers of people employed in them.

The sounds of industrial processes, which must have been ubiquitous in some parts of Victorian Britain, are also largely absent from the later and more scholarly dialect surveys. Only the old extractive labour of mining and quarrying is mentioned much alongside the expressions used in fields, market towns and fishing villages. It is rural life which the surveys represent the best and from this we can gain insights into not just what was heard but also how it was heard.

There are words for sounds emanating from the earth or of things coming into contact with it: *balk*, *squashle*, *gludder*, *slosh*, *snurr*, *elf-mill*. Where the land meets the sea there can be heard the *hush*, *labb*, *drow*, *brimtud*, *scale*, and the *sing-of-the-shore*. The wind might *soo*, *whew*, *gurl*, *ruddy*, *huffle* or *rave*, and if it is said to *sob* or the *hiren* is heard, then its sound is being used to predict what the weather will do next.

The vocalisations of domesticated animals are also subject to great scrutiny. Dogs don't just bark or growl, but can also *baff*, *hask*, *snook*, *channer*, *churr*, *whink* and *yalder*. Horses *snicker*, *quelch*, *winnow* and indulge in *ninny-niawing*, while cattle *wuther*, *hoost*, *mourn*, *njoag* and *puist*. Even the characteristic sounds of some plants are noted, as are the simple musical instruments made from them by children: the *pee-wit*, *skirlag*, *speawker* and others.

Individual human noises appear with coughing and sneezing, tones of voice, stomach rumbles and death rattles. Social discourse ranges from the covert sounds of the *cuddlie*, *lunning* and the calculations of the *darking-dog* through words for whining, wheedling, false laughter and high-falutin' speech to the collective uproar of the *skimmington*, *randivoose* and *hurlie-go-thorow*.

Attentiveness towards sound appears also in the omens of the *coffin*, *dead-drap*, *heather-bleat* and *seven whistlers*, all believed to foretell imminent death or other misfortune. Divination through sound is conducted by *alveromancy* and *gastromancy*, and the Scottish Highland practice of *taghairm* suggests an ancient, pre-Christian ritual. Here, too, are the unseen and often malign apparitions of the *bucca*, *striker*, *padfoot*, *clap-cans* and *colt-pixie*, imagined vessels into which the uncertainties of rural life could be poured.

The country was being transformed. Clearances, enclosures and new agricultural techniques were driving labourers and tenant farmers towards the cities and factories, or else overseas. Technology progressed from bells, primitive alarms and bird-scaring devices to steam whistles, internal combustion engines and the whole early apparatus of sound recording and reproduction. Knowledge of the music of other cultures was gathered and systematically catalogued, just as the dialect words and folklore of our own country began to be collected in earnest, once the possibility of their eventual disappearance was recognised.

We live on the other side of a great sonic extinction. What came before now appears as vital and fascinating, a world inhabited by people who listened to their surroundings more than we do, and who made the streets alive with their voices.

A

ABENG. A cow's horn used as a musical instrument and for signalling, especially among the Maroons. It is blown, not from the end, but from a mouth-hole on the concave side. Another hole, located at the small end, is stopped with the thumb and so gives a variation of about a tone. Late 19C. *Jamaica*.

ACOUASM. A ringing noise heard inside the head. 19C.

ACOUSTIC-CHAIR. A chair the size of a large library one, with a high back, to which are affixed two barrels for sound, and at the extremity of each is a perforated plate which collects sound into a paraboloid vase from any part of the room. The instrument thus gathers sound, and impresses it more sensibly by giving to it a small quantity of air. The convex end of the vase serves to reflect the voice, and renders it more distinct. Mid 19C.

ACOUSTICAL-TELEGRAPH. A telegraph in which musical pipes are acted upon by wind for the purpose of communicating intelligence. The passage between a reservoir of pressurised air and the pipe is closed by a valve which, when acted upon by an electro-magnet, opens and allows the passage of wind to the pipe. Long and short sounds may thus be made to follow each other according to the letters of Morse's telegraph. Mid 19c.

ACOUSTICON. A device, taking several different forms, intended to assist hearing by amplifying sound. 17c.

ACTINOPHONE. An apparatus for the production of sound by the action of the actinic, or ultraviolet, rays. Late 19c.

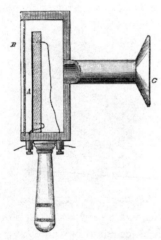

AEOLIAN-HARP. An instrument with the strings placed on a hollow sounding-board, formed of a wedge shape, and fixed to a spindle supported on a suitable framework. Near the sides of the sounding-board are placed curved wind conductors which collect a large quantity of wind and concentrate it upon the strings or wires. The spindle allows the aeolian harp to turn and catch the wind at any point of the compass. Mid 19c.

AEROPHONE. A class of musical instruments in which a body of air is caused to vibrate without recourse to strings or membranes; a device of Edison's for amplifying speech sounds outdoors. 19c.

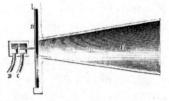

AGITATOR. A door-knocker or bell-rope. Mid 19c. *London*.

AICH. An echo. Early 19c. *Scotland*.

ALMANIE-WHISTLE. A child's musical instrument; a flageolet of a very small size. Early 19c. *Aberdeens*.

ALVEROMANCY. A method of divination performed by attending to and interpreting certain sounds, so that the loudness of the sound is taken to indicate the severity of a predicted event, and from its proximity how soon the event will come to pass. Late 19C.

AMERICAN-DEVIL. A hooter or steam whistle; used in place of a bell for summoning to work. Late 19C.

AMMONIAPHONE. An instrument said to improve the quality of the singing and speaking voice, being an apparatus for inhaling peroxide of hydrogen and free ammonia. Late 19C.

THE PEERLESS "QUEEN OF SONG"
APPROVED OF
THE AMMONIAPHONE.

AMPHORIC. Produced by, or indicating, a cavity in the lungs, and giving a sound like that produced by blowing into an empty decanter; as in amphoric respiration. Early 19C.

ANACAMPTICS. The science of reflected sounds. 18C.

ANACLASTIC-GLASSES. Sonorous phials or glasses, chiefly made in Germany. On gently sucking the air out of the glass, the bottom gives way with a loud crack, turning from convex to concave. The process is reversed, with no less noise, on breathing back into the glass. 18C.

ANGEL'S-WHISPER. A bugle call in a military camp or barracks. Early 20C. *United States.*

ANTIGUGGLER. A crooked tube of metal, to be introduced into the neck of a bottle for drawing out the liquid without disturbing the sediment or causing a gurgling noise. 18C.

ARGUTE. Shrill in sound. 18C.

ARMISONANT. Rustling with weapons; resounding with arms. 18C.

ARRIVAL. The sound made by an approaching artillery shell. Early 20C.

ASONIA. Deafness to specific pitches of sound. 19C.

AUDILE. Of or relating to hearing; a person who is more disposed to the auditory than the other senses. Late 19C.

AUDIPHONE. An instrument which, when placed against the

teeth, conveys sound to the auditory nerve and enables the deaf to hear more or less distinctly. Late 19C.

AUNT. The hare, *Lepus europaeus*; so called from its supposed cry when startled. Late 19C. *Essex.*

AURICLE. A form of hearing instrument worn on the head in pairs, each consisting of a metal cone with a large sound-collector doubled on itself. The slender end of the cone terminates in a nipple, through which sound is conveyed faithfully to the ear. Mid 19C.

AUSCULTATION. A medical examination by listening either directly with the ear applied to parts of the body, as the abdomen; or with the stethoscope, in order to distinguish sounds recognized as a sign of health or of disease. Early 19C.

AUTOPHONY. An auscultatory process, which consists in noting the tone of the observer's own voice, while he speaks holding his head close to the patient's chest. Early 19C.

B

BABBLE. The noise made by hounds when they give tongue before being sure of the scent. 17c. *N. England*.

BABY-CRYING. The bugle call emitted to summon those who have broken the army's disciplinary code. Early 20c.

BACK-SCRATCHER. A wooden toy on the principle of a watchman's rattle, which, drawn down the back, sounds like the ripping up of cloth. Much in favour at fairs and in crowds, its use in London has been prohibited by police order. Early 20c.

BADGER'S-BAND. The clashing of kettles, pans, &c., in front of the home of an obnoxious person; a rural form of punishment for notorious offenders. Late 19c. *Hants*.

BADGY-FIDDLER. A boy trumpeter or bugler in the army. 19c.

BAFF. A suppressed bark of a dog. Late 19c. *Yorks*.

BAGPIPE. A talkative or long-winded person. Early 20c. *United States*.

BAIRGE. Of the voice used loudly either in speaking, weeping, or calling; a person who raises his voice in a strong, loud manner. Late 19C. *Banffs.*

BAINBRIDGE-HORN. The horn blown in Bainbridge each evening at nine o'clock between the 28th of September and Shrove Tuesday. It was first sounded in medieval times to guide travellers to safety. 19C. *Yorks.*

BAL. Loud talking or chatter. Late 19C. *Cornwall.*

BALK. Loose ground which sounds hollow when struck. Late 19C. *Cornwall.*

BALLAD-BASKET. A street singer of ballads, &c. 19C.

BALL'S-BULL. As, like Ball's bull, said of a person with no ear for music. The expression alludes to a proverbial bull which kicked a fiddler over a bridge. Mid 19C.

BALLYHOO. Shouted advertising by a fairground barker or *spieler.* Early 20C. *United States.*

BALLYWRAG. To scold or accuse someone loudly with obnoxious language. Late 19C.

BAMBLUSTERATE. A noisy attempt to hoax or confuse another person 19C.

BANDA. The lead drum in a *Cumina* cult group of drums. Early 20C. *Jamaica.*

BANDER. One of a band of musicians. Late 19C. *Yorks.*

BANDOG-AND-BEDLAM. As, to speak bandog-and-bedlam: to speak in a rage, as a madman. 19C.

BANDORE. A musical instrument with strings; an old variety of zither. 18C. *Gloucs.*

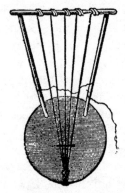

BANGING-OUT. A noisy ceremony marking the completion of an apprenticeship in a factory or other place of work, accompanied by the banging of tools. Early 20C.

BANJEE. A band of music. 19C. *Anglo-Indian.*

BANNAG. A ballad, especially one sung or shouted on the night of the 11th of November, Hallow

Eve, by groups of young people. 19C. *Isle of Man.*

BANTER-SING. A group song raised by men working among the yam-hills and at other labour. The songs may often refer in a satirical way to local events and persons. Early 20C. *Jamaica.*

BANYAN-FIGHT. A furious row which, despite being vociferous, never rises to blows or bloodshed. Late 19C. *Anglo-Indian.*

BARBLY. Babble, noise. 19C.

BARGUEST. A supernatural apparition in animal shape, such as a large dog, donkey, calf, &c., which makes a terrible shriek or roar. 18C. *Yorks.*

BARK. The short, sharp cry uttered by a fox when it is inclined to copulate at rutting-time. Mid 19C. *Lancs.*

BARKER. A man employed to cry at fairgrounds and by shops to entice people inside. 19*C.*

BARKERS. Military slang for sausages; so called from the noise made while frying. Early 20c.

BARKING-CREEK. Persons troubled with a short cough are said to have been there, or else to 'Barkingside'. Early 19C. *London.*

BARKING-IRONS. Pistols, especially large duelling pistols; so called in allusion to the report on explosion. Early 19C.

BARREL-ALARM. A kind of fire alarm which is set off by the burning and destruction of a thin cord attached to a barrel. Without the arresting action of the cord, the barrel begins to rotate under the influence of a weight suspended from it by a pulley. The spinning motion is conveyed to a crown wheel, which in turn causes a hammer to strike a bell repeatedly. 18c.

BARRIKIN. High-flown speech, cant, jargon, gibberish. Mid 19C. *London.*

BARST. A loud noise. Late 19C. *Cheshire.*

BAUTER, BAWTHER. To tread clumsily and with noise. Late 19C. *Yorks.*

BAWK, BAWK-AIT. To make an abrupt bellowing noise, as when animals are suddenly frightened. Late 19C. *Cheshire.*

BAWL. To read aloud. Late 19C. *Sussex.*

BAWLER. A hawker who cries his wares in the street. Late 19C. *London.*

BAWSE. To cry out. 19C.

BAZER. A bass singer in a choir. Late 19C. *Isle of Man.*

BAZOO. A horn; loud and conceited talk. Early 20C. *United States.*

BEAL. To bellow or roar as cattle do; to raise the voice. 18C. *N. England.*

BEAR-A-PARL. To join vocally or musically in a harmony. Late 19C. *E. Anglia.*

BEATING-DADDY-MAMMY. The practice of the elements of military drum-beating. Early 20C.

BED-BELL. A waggish custom at weddings to hang a bell under the matrimonial bed: 'Tinkle, tinkle, goes the Bell under the Bed, whilst Time and Touch they keep'. 17C.

BEE-BAW. To lull to sleep; a lullaby. Early 19C. *N. England.*

BEEF. A bawl or yell, especially made by the performers in a musical-hall or low theatre. 19C.

BEEF-HEART. Rhyming slang: the act of flatulence. 'Beef-hearts' is also slang for beans, indicating an association of the two terms. 19C. *London.*

BEER-O. The cry when an artisan does a something, or omits to do a something, the result of which in either case being a fine to be paid in drink. The exclamation is taken up by the whole shop, or rather was, as the custom is now obsolete. Late 19C.

BELCH. Beer, especially poor beer, because of its liability to cause eructation. Early 19C. *Yorks.*

BELDER. To bellow, as a bull or cow; to cry loudly or roar, as a hurt or cross-tempered child. Early 19c. *N. England.*

BELG. To roar, bellow. Mid 19c. *Somerset.*

BELL. A song, especially one sung in the street in the hope of payment, diminutive of 'bellow'. 19c.

BELL-HARMONICA. A flattened tube or elliptical chamber of glass placed in the interior of the body of a violin. A bow-shaped bar of lancewood is placed transversely across the body of the instrument above the glass chamber. Violins formed and fitted in this way give a very superior tone. Mid 19c.

BELL-HOSS. The leading horse in a pack-horse train, with a bell hung round its neck. 19c. *Yorks.*

BELL-HOUR. Meal-time in a factory. Late 19c.

BELL-TINKER. A thrashing, or the threat of one, as severe as when a tinker makes a kettle ring with the blows he gives it. Mid 19c. *Staffs., Lancs. and Yorks.*

BELL-PLOW. A wagon pulled by a team of belled horses. Late 19c. *Dorset.*

BELL-SHEEP. A sheep selected by a shearer just as the breakfast or dinner bell is rung, in order to improve his daily tally. Early 20c. *Australia.*

BELL-SOLLER. The ringing chamber or loft for bells in a church. 16c. *E. Anglia.*

BELLERING-CAKE. A cake in which the plums are so far apart they are supposed to 'beller' or bellow when they wish to converse. Late 19c. *Schoolboys' slang.*

BELLOCK. To cry like a frightened child. Early 19c. *Wilts.*

BELLOWER. A town-crier. 18c.

BELLY-CLAPPER. A dinner bell. Mid 19c.

BELOWNDER. The noise of a heavy fall. Late 19c. *Shrops.*

BENDER. A musical instrument made of a bent stick, the ends of which are restrained by a slip of dried grass. The upper part is gently compressed between the lips, and to which the breath gives a soft and pleasing vibration. The other end is graduated by means of a slender stick, so producing a trembling, querulous and delightful harmony. 18C. *Jamaica.*

BERLUE. Noisy commotion, hullaballoo. Early 20C. *United States.*

BIBLE-MILL. A public house, especially one in which raucous conversation is the norm. 19C. *London.*

BILLINGSGATE. Foul, loud and vituperative language; so called from the abuse for which the fish-women at Billingsgate market were once widely renowned. 17C. *London.*

BILLY-YN-TWEET. The meadow pipit, *Anthus pratensis*; so called from its twittering. Early 20C. *Isle of Man.*

BIM-BOMS. Church bells; from this applied to anything hanging, as icicles, &c. Late 19C. *Somerset.*

BINNER. A quick movement accompanied by much noise; a sounding blow. Early 19C. *N.E. Scotland.*

BIRD. The hissing of an actor to indicate disapproval, in imitation of the hostile hissing of a goose. 19C.

BIRD-CLACKER. A rattle with which to frighten away birds from a corn field. Late 19C. *Dorset.*

BIRR. To make, or move with, a whirring noise, as of wheels in motion. Early 19C. *Scotland and Northumb.*

BLACK-SANCTUS. A burlesque hymn or anthem; rough music. Late 19C.

BLADDER-MOUTH. A noisy, blustering fool. Late 19C. *Somerset.*

BLARE. To cry; the crying of a baby. Early 20c. *United States.*

BLASS. An accent of speech. Early 20c. *Isle of Man.*

BLAT. To cry, as a calf or sheep; to bleat; to make a senseless noise; to talk without consideration. Mid 19c.

BLEAK-BLEAK. The cry of the hare. Late 19c. *Aberdeens.*

BLEARE. To low as a cow; to cry loudly as a fretful child. Late 19c. *Dorset.*

BLEATING. The noise made by the wings of the snipe, *Gallinago gallinago,* whilst in flight. Late 19c. *Hants.*

BLETHER. To make a noise like a calf; to make a 'faal' noise. Late 19c. *Yorks.*

BLETHER-BAISE. A musical instrument, the strings of which are stretched across a bladder to serve as a sounding-board. Late 19c. *N. England.*

BLETHERING-TAM. The whitethroat, *Sylvia communis*; so called from its rapid and voluble song. Late 19c. *Renfrews.*

BLIMP. A dirigible airship without an internal framework or a keel; so called from the hollow, echoing sound made by flicking the airship's taut fabric with a finger. Early 20c.

BLIND-HARPER. A beggar who, whilst pretending to be blind, plays the harp. 19c.

BLITTER-BLATTER. A term used to express a rattling, irregular noise. Early 19c. *Dumfries.*

BLOCHER. To make a gurgling noise whilst coughing. Late 19c. *Angus and Perths.*

BLODDER. Of liquor: to flow with a gurgling sound out of a vessel. Late 19c. *Westmor.*

BLOUT. The noise made by liquids boiling over a hot flame; the noisy eruption of a liquid substance. Early 19c. *Scotland.*

BLOW. Sailors' slang: to boast, from the sound when a whale blows water from the nostrils, with much noise. 19c.

BLOWING-FOR-BURNS. Breathing onto a burn or wound with the accompaniment of a form of words. Late 19C. *Co. Durham.*

BLUE-MURDERS. Desperate cries of terror or alarm. 19C.

BLUGGAN-SNAIE. Literally, a 'ball of thread'; the name given to a tune which is tedious and as long in coming to an end as a ball of thread. 19C. *Isle of Man.*

BOBBERY. A noise, squabble, loud disturbance; from a Hindu expression of surprise. Late 19C. *Anglo-Indian.*

BOBBERY-PACK. A pack of hounds of different breeds, with which young officers hunt jackals; so called from the noise and disturbance such a pack are apt to raise. Late 19C. *Anglo-Indian.*

BOILED-BELL. Ribald term for Port Glasgow used by the inhabitants of Greenock. It alludes to a bell presented to Port Glasgow which occasioned such pride that it was painted repeatedly, so that eventually it ceased to ring. The townsfolk then had to boil the paint off. 19C. *Renfrews.*

BOLCH. The sound caused by a heavy fall. Late 19C. *Midlands and N. England.*

BOLDER. A loud, resonant noise or report. Mid 19C. *Cumber. and Yorks.*

BOM. A large American snake; so called from the sound it is alleged to make. Late 19C. *United States.*

BOMBILATION. A continuous humming sound; a booming as of cannon-fire. 17C.

BOOFF. To strike, especially with the hand, so as to cause a hollow sound. Late 19C. *Fife.*

BOOHOO-OWL. The name given by the Appalachians to the hoot owl, *Strix varia*; so called in imitation of its mournful note. Early 20C. *United States.*

BOOMER. The North American

mountain beaver, *Aplodontia rufa*; so called because it is said to make a curious booming call. Early 20C. *United States.*

BOOTH-BURSTER. A stentorian, strong-voiced actor. 19C.

BOP. To throw anything down with a resounding noise. Late 19C. *Kent.*

BORBORYGMUS. A rumbling or gurgling noise produced by wind in the bowels. 18C.

BOSH. To bark, as a dog. Late 19C. *English Gypsy.*

BOSHERO. A fiddle-player. Late 19C. *English Gypsy.*

BOSHOMENGRO. A fiddle. Late 19C. *English Gypsy.*

BOTTLE-BUMP. The bittern, *Botaurus stellaris*; so called in imitation of its dull, hollow note which may be carried a great distance across the marshlands. Late 19C. *Yorks. and E. Anglia.*

BOTTLER. A collector of money for a musical band; a street musician. 19C.

BOTUTO. An ancient form of trumpet, used by the Indians near the river Orinoco. It was made of baked clay and was commonly three to four feet long; but some trumpets of this kind were of enormous size. The botuto with two bellies was usually made thicker than that with three bellies and emitted a deeper sound, which is described as having been really terrific. These trumpets were used on occasions of mourning and during funeral dances.

BOUNCE. An imitation of the sound of an explosion or the discharge of a gun. 16C.

BOUK. In mining, a report made by the cracking of the strata owing to the extraction of coal beneath; also the noise made by the escape of gas under great pressure. Late 19C. *Co. Durham and Northum.*

BOX-OF-TOYS. Rhyming slang: a noise, typically a loud one. Early 20C. *London.*

BRABBLEMENT. The noise of people quarrelling. Mid 19C. *N. England.*

BRAG. An apparition or bogey that makes hideous noises in the night. Mid 19C. *Northum.*

BRAGGING. The sound made by the grouse. Late 19C. *Yorks.*

BRATTLE. A loud clattering or rattling noise. 18C. *Scotland and N. England.*

BRAWL. To make a loud confused noise, as the water of a rapid stream running over stones. Early 19C.

BREAD-AND-CHEESE. Rhyming slang: to sneeze; a sneeze. Early 20C. *London.*

BREE. The gadfly, *Estrus bovis*; so called from the sound of the insect's wings, enough of itself to set a herd of oxen or cows half wild. Mid 19C. *Cleveland.*

BREEZE. A short brisk scolding bout involving one or more voices. Early 19C. *London.*

BRIMTUD. The sound of waves crashing on a shore. Late 19C. *Orkney and Shetland.*

BRITISH-LYRE. An instrument with seven wire strings, the notes of which are produced by being struck with hammers contained inside the body of the lyre, and which in turn are actuated by seven keys fixed to the outside. 18C.

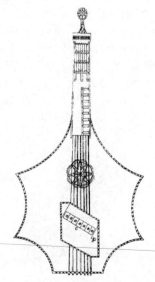

BRONCHOPHONY. A modification of the voice sounds, by which they are intensified and heightened in pitch; observed during medical auscultation of the chest in cases of intro-thoracic disease. Mid 19c.

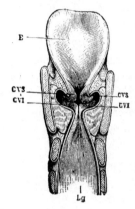

BROOL. A deep murmuring or humming sound, produced by a multitudinous source. Mid 19c.

BRUIT. An abnormal sound of several kinds, heard by a doctor during an auscultatory examination. Mid 19c.

BUBBLER. A fish of the Ohio river; so called from the noise it makes. Late 19c. *United States.*

BUBBLY-MARY. The wompoo pigeon, *Ptilinopus magnificus*; so called for its distinctive 'bubbling' cry. Early 20c. *Australia.*

BUCCA, BUCCA-BOO. In the west of England, a hollow noise on the sea-coast was referred to a spirit or goblin called Bucca, and was supposed to foretell a shipwreck. Peculiar marks on rocks were alleged to be the remains of fishing nets which the Bucca had attempted to steal, only for them to turn to stone when the Bucca heard a church choir sing the Creed. 19c. *Cornwall.*

BUCCINAL. Shaped or sounding like a trumpet. Mid 19c.

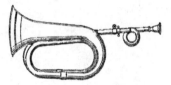

BUCK. The sound made by a stone falling into water. Late 19c. *Scotland and Orkney.*

BUCK-STICK. One who prattles or chatters. From Hindu *bakna*, to prattle. Late 19c. *Anglo-Indian.*

BUF. The sound made in belching. *Middle English.*

BUFFET. To deaden the sound of bells by muffling the clapper. 18c.

BUGLE. The nose; so called from the sound of it being blown. Early 20c. *Polari.*

BULBUL. Any one of several bird species of the family *Pycnonotidae*; derived from the Persian *bulbul* or nightingale. The name is no doubt intended to be echoic of the bird's note. Late 19c. *Anglo-Indian*.

BULE. To weep with continuous noise; to drawl in singing. Early 19c. *Roxburghs*.

BULL-RATTLE. The bladder campion, *Silene latifolia*; so called for the sound made by the dry inflated calyx of this species. Late 19c. *Bucks*.

BULL-ROARER. A contrivance consisting of a slat of wood tied to the end of a thong or string, with which the slat is whirled so as to cause an intermittent roaring noise. It is used principally as a toy, and among some races in certain religious rites. Late 19c.

BULL'S-NOON. Midnight; so called from the habit of bulls to bellow at night time, as they rush forth on their adventures following the evening's rumination, as if it were broad noon-day. Late 19c. *E. Anglia*.

BUM-BASS. The cello or violoncello. Late 19c. *Yorks*.

BUM-CLOCK. A humming flying beetle. 18c. *Ayrshire*.

BUMBELEERY-BIZZ. A cry used by children when they see cows startling, in order to excite them to run about with greater violence. Late 19c. *Lanarks*.

BUMBLE. To muffle, as of church bells at a funeral. Late 19c. *E. Anglia*.

BUMBLE-JAR. In the Royal Navy, a ship chaplain's harmonium. 19c.

BUMMER. A bumble-bee, bluebottle fly; any humming insect; a child's toy made with a piece of twine and small circular disc, usually of tin, which produces a humming noise when spun rapidly. Early 19c.

BUMMLAN. The act of reading in a low, indistinct voice, or of singing or playing on a musical instrument in a blundering way. Late 19c. *Scotland*.

BUMP. The noise made by the bittern. 16c.

BUNG. To emit a buzzing or twanging sound as of something thrown through the air. 19c.

BURN-WHISPERING. A cure for burns, in which the following verse must be whispered close to the portion of skin so affected: 'There came two angels from the north. One was Fire and one was Frost. Out Fire, in Frost. In the name of the Father, Son and Holy Ghost.' Late 19c. *Sussex*.

BUSHMAN'S-CLOCK. The kookaburra, a bird of the genus *Dacelo*; so called from its loud call made early in the morning. Early 20c. *Australia*.

BUZZARD, BUZZERT. The cockchafer, *Melolontha melolontha*; so called from the buzzing, clattering sound made in flight. Mid 19c. *E. Anglia and Lancs*.

BUZZED. To be buzzed: to be killed by a bullet, from the 'buzz' of a bullet. Early 20c.

BUZZER. A road-motor of any kind; so called from the noise made during progress. Early 20c.

C

CABBAG. Stuttering or stammering. Early 20C. *Isle of Man.*

CACHINNATION. Raucous and loud laughter. 17C.

CACKLING-CHETE. A cock or capon; literally, a cackling thing. 17C. *Thieves' slang.*

CAIM. To make loud noises in derision. Late 19C. *Staffs. and Shrops.*

CAKE. Of geese: to raise a cackling. Early 19C. *Yorks.*

CALEVEERING. Running about in a noisy, boisterous manner. Mid 19C. *Co. Durham.*

CALL. The instrument with which a Punch-and-Judy man patters. Mid 19C. *London.*

CALLER. The noise of many voices speaking. Late 19C. *English Gypsy.*

CALLIOPE. An instrument producing musical notes by means of steam-whistles, played by a keyboard. Mid 19C.

CALLITHUMP. A somewhat riotous parade, accompanied with the blowing of tin horns, and other discordant noises. Early 20C. *United States.*

CANARY. A music-hall chorus-singer typically situated amongst the public in the gallery. Late 19C. *London.*

CANOROUS. Musical, melodious, as of song-birds. 17c.

CANTER. To talk too fast or too much. Early 20c. *United States.*

CANTERBURY-BELL. The common garden name for *Campanula medium*; so called after the small bells which medieval pilgrims to Canterbury fixed to the trappings of their horses. 16c.

CANTILLORY-REALISM. A way of singing in which the sounds suggest the words sung. Very open to ridicule, but intended quite gravely. At once burlesqued: where 'kiss' was used, the lips were smacked. If 'thunder' came in the words, the singer used all his bass voice, &c. Late 19c.

CAPROUSE. A great noise, uproar. Late 19c. *Cornwall.*

CAPSTAN-STEP. The time kept by the old ship's fiddler for capstan work. 19c.

CARTS. A pair of boots, generally those of a noble size; so called in reference to the noise a young navvy can make with them, supposedly equal to that of the passing waggon. Late 19c. *London.*

CARWHILLAG. Literally, a 'song fly'; a fly or bluebottle. Early 20c. *Isle of Man.*

CATAPHONICS. That part of acoustics which treats of reflected sounds or echoes. 17c.

CAT-CALL. A kind of whistle or squeaking instrument used in playhouses on the part of the audience to express impatience or disapprobation. Early 19c.

CATERWAULING. Applied derisively to inharmonious singing; also love-making, from the noise

of cats similarly engaged. Early
19C.

CATGUT-SCRAPERS. An orch-
estra; any group of players on
stringed instruments. Late 19C.
London.

CATOUSE. An uproar, noise,
rumpus. Early 20C. *United States.*

CAWDY-MAWDY. The curlew,
Numenius arquata. The bird has
two cries, the first being a whistle
of two syllables, resembling the
name 'cur-lew'. The second is
harsh and guttural, hence 'cawdy
mawdy'. Late 19C. *N. England.*

CAWK. To cry out, make a noise
like a hen when disturbed on her
nest. Late 19C. *Wilts.*

CELESTINA. A key instrument
generally shaped like a harpsi-
chord, with one, two or more wire
or catgut strings to a note. The
tone is produced by the motion of
a band of silk, flax or leather
against the string, effected by
means of a spring or traddle. 18C.

CENSIONER. A judge at a bell-
ringing match, who is placed in a
room isolated from other persons,
listens to the ringing, marks the
blunders, and gives judgment.
Late 19C. *Yorks.*

CHACKLE. A clattering or

rattling noise. Late 19C. *Worcs. and
Gloucs.*

CHACKLING. The noise made
by a hen after laying an egg. Late
19C. *Berks.*

CHAFFLE. To mutter. Late 19C.
Yorks.

CHALUMEAU. A wooden pipe
played by shepherds. 18C.

CHAMADE. A military signal
inviting to parley, made by the
beating of a drum or a trumpet-
call. 17C.

CHANG. A loud and confused
noise, uproar; the cry of a pack of
hounds. Early 19C. *Scotland and
N. England.*

CHANNER. The suppressed
noise between a bark and a whine
which a dog makes when watch-
ing for a rat. Late 19C. *Lincs.*

CHANTER, CHAUNTER. A street
seller and singer of ballads. Mid
19C. *London.*

CHANTEY. A song sung by sailors at their work. The music is to a certain extent traditional; the words, which are commonly unfit for ears polite, are traditional likewise. The words and music are divided into two distinct parts: the chantey proper, which is delivered by a single voice, with or without a fiddle, and the refrain and chorus, which are sung with much straining and tugging, and with peculiar breaks and strange and melancholy stresses, by a number of men engaged in the actual performance of some piece of bodily labour. 19C.

CHANTING-KEN. A music-hall. 19C. *London.*

CHARK. To make a grating noise as the teeth do in biting any gritty substance; to make a grinding, grunting noise. Early 19C. *Dumfries.*

CHARLEY. The Navy's reveille bugle-call which has these words: 'Charley! Charley! get up and wash yourself. Charley! Charley! lash up and stow'. Early 20C.

CHARM. A confused, murmuring noise; the sound of many voices all talking noisily. Mid 19C. *Midlands and S. England.*

CHARM-BIRDS. To catch birds by night by carrying a light and ringing a bell. The birds suffer themselves to be taken by the hand. Late 19C. *Somerset.*

CHAT. A genus of small birds in the thrush family, of which the wheatear is a familiar example; so called from its note, crying 'chat' four or five times when it begins to fly. Late 19C. *Midlands and S. England.*

CHATTER. The peculiar noise made by the hen before she sits. Late 19C. *Northants.*

CHATTER-MAG. A chattering magpie; a chatterbox. Late 19C. *Dorset.*

CHATTER-PIE. The magpie, *Pica pica.* Early 20C. *Somerset.*

CHAUK. The jackdaw, *Corvus monedula*; so called in imitation of its cawing noise. Late 19C. *Devon and Cornwall.*

CHAUNTER-CULLS. A body of men who used to write satirical or libellous ballads on any person, or body of persons, for a consideration. 7s. 6d. was the usual fee, and in three hours the ballad might be heard in St. Paul's Churchyard, or some other public spot. Early 19C. *London.*

CHAVISH. A chattering or prattling noise of many persons speaking together; a noise made by a flock of birds. 17C. *S. England.*

CHEEPART. A person of small stature with a shrill voice. Late 19C. *Banffs.*

CHEEPER. The plant bog iris, *Iris pseudacorus*; so called because children make a shrill noise with its leaves; a young partridge or grouse, before it has attained its powers of flight, and whose cry of alarm is more acute than that of the full-grown bird. Late 19C. *Scotland and N. England.*

CHEEPS. Squeaking or creaking shoes. Late 19C. *Scotland.*

CHEESE-BIRD. The yellow-hammer, *Emberiza citrinella*; so called because of the transliterated rendering of its song as 'a little bit of bread and no cheese'. Early 20C. S*omerset.*

CHEET. To creak, make a slight noise; to squeak, call out. Mid 19C. *Yorks.*

CHEETER. A young pigeon for the first four weeks of its existence; so called from its plaintive calls. Late 19c. *Yorks.*

CHELP. To produce a chirping or squeaking sound, as of a bird; to yelp; of children: to chatter or prattle Mid 19c. *Midlands and N. England.*

CHERRY-CLACK. A contrivance placed in a cherry tree to frighten away the birds, generally in the form of a small windmill with wooden sails. As it revolves, the sails strike in rapid succession against a piece of wood, and make a considerable noise. Late 19c. *Cheshire.*

CHERUBINE-MINOR. A keyed instrument resembling a pianoforte, in which a harp, an organ and a series of glass bells are all combined in a harmonious fashion. Mid 19c.

CHEVY. In field-sports, the blast of a horn, the notes of which are intelligible to the sportsman. Early 19c.

CHEWALLOP. An onomatopoeic representation, it is thought, of the sound of an object falling heavily to the ground or into water. Late 19c.

CHICK-CHACKER. The wheatear, *Saxicola oenanthe*; so called in imitation of its common clear note, which is not unlike the sound made in breaking stones with a hammer. Early 19c. *Cornwall and Devon.*

CHICKERING. Chirping, as of a cricket, sparrow, &c. Early 19c. *Lincs. and Northants.*

CHI-IKE. Originally a distance call of the Red Indians, since copied by American trappers. Now often sent along the street by urchins as an unfriendly greeting to a 'toff'. Late 19c.

CHILD-CROWING. The crowing noise made by children affected with spasms of the laryngeal muscles; false croup. Early 19c.

CHIMCHEAY. A mincing kind of talk. Late 19c. *Dorset.*

CHIN-MUSIC. The noise made

by children crying; too much talk, chattering, scolding; impertinence. Mid 19C.

CHINK. To rustle as hay, &c. does when dry. Late 19C. *Derbys. and Notts.*

CHINK-CHINK. The chaffinch, *Fringilla coelebs*; so called from its ringing, musical call-note. Late 19C. *Shrops.*

CHINK-COUGH. The whooping-cough; so called from the sharp chinking sound by which it is accompanied. Mid 19C. *Lancs.*

CHINKERS. Money; so called from the sound produced by loose coins. Early 19C.

CHIPPER. To chirp, as a bird. A metathesis of 'chirrup'. Late 19C. *Somerset.*

CHIRL. To chirp, sing as a bird; to warble; to emit a slight and melancholy sound. Early 19C. *Scotland.*

CHIRM. Clamour; a confused, intermingled hum; buzzing or humming. 17C.

CHIRPER. A stage door blackmailer; if money be refused them, they go into the auditorium and begin to hoot, hiss, and groan at the performer. Late 19C.

CHIRPLE. To twitter as a swallow does; a twittering note. Late 19C. *N. Scotland.*

CHIRRUP. To applaud or cheer a singer, speaker, &c., especially in a music-hall and for a consideration. 19C. *London.*

CHISSUP. To sneeze; a word evidently formed from the sound. Late 19C. *Yorks.*

CHITTER. To twitter, chirp. Early 20C. *United States.*

CHITTER-HI-TI. The sedge-warbler, *Acrocephalus phragmitis*; so called from its twittering or chirping. Late 19C. *Lanarks.*

CHITTER-WAOW. The caterwauling of cats. Late 19C. *Cumber.*

CHITTERLING. A rapid chattering noise made by the swallow, *Hirundo rustica*. Late 19C. *N. Ireland.*

CHIVEY. A shout, a cry; a cheer; to hunt down with shouts. Early 19C.

CHOICE-AND-CHEEP. The leaf warbler or chiffchaff, *Phylloscopus collybita*; so called from its constantly repeated short, hurried note. Late 19C. *Devon.*

CHOICE-RIOT. A horrid noise, such as the festive sounding of marrowbones and cleavers by butchers and their apprentices; the term may be used satirically. Late 19C.

CHOWTER. To grumble, growl; a female fish-vendor, implying a voluble and clamorous disputant. Early 19C. *Devon.*

CHUCK-UP. Applause or cheering. When a ship has been in action and covered herself with glory, her sister ships usually give her a 'chuck up' as she comes in harbour. Early 20C.

CHUCKLE. To scold, brawl, make a noise; to rattle. Late 19C. *Derbys. and Worcs.*

CHUCKLING. A salt-making term, expressive of the noise made by a pan boiling in any part not over the fire. Late 19C. *Cheshire.*

CHUG-A-LUG. Imitative of the gurgling sound made by a person when drinking in large gulps; a toast or exhortation to drink. Early 20C. *United States.*

CHUGGER. A type of fishing lure which, when pulled across the surface of the water, produces a characteristic gurgling sound. Early 20C. *United States.*

CHUMMAGE. An old custom amongst prisoners when a fresh reprobate is admitted to their number, consisting of a rough music made with pokers, tongs, sticks, and saucepans. Early 19C.

CHURCHING-MICE. To murmur in an undertone. Late 19C. *Shrops.*

CHURCHMAN. A clergyman who is a good reader or has a powerful voice; also a person who reads the responses loudly in church. Late 19C. *Worcs, E. Anglia and S. England.*

CHURR. The call of the nightjar or the missel-thrush, a whirring sound; a low, deep noise as of the subdued growling of a dog. 18C. *N. England and Scotland.*

CHUTTERING. A subdued chirping. Late 19C. *Yorks.*

CLAAG. A clamorous sound of many birds or voices. Late 19C. *Shetland.*

CLABBER-MOUTHED. Of a person: to be silent, reluctant to speak. Early 20C. *United States.*

CLACK. The noise made by a hen, goose, &c.; chatter, noisy talk. Mid 19C.

CLACK-DISH. A wooden dish carried by beggars, having a movable cover which they clacked to attract attention. 17C.

CLACK-VALVE. A valve; especially one hinged at one edge, which, when raised from its seat, falls with a clacking sound. 17C.

CLACKER. A wooden rattle used to frighten away birds. Late 19C. *Cornwall.*

CLACKET. Chatter, racket, din. Early 19C. *S. and W. England.*

CLAM. The noise produced in ringing a chime of bells at once. 18C.

CLAM-SHELLS. A wild sound supposed to be made by goblins in the air. Early 19C. *Scotland.*

CLANJANDERING. A worrying noise. Late 19C. *Essex.*

CLAP. A flat instrument of iron like a box with tongue and handle, used for making proclamations through a town instead of a drum or handbell. Hence 'clapman', a public crier. 18C. *Scotland.*

CLAP-A-BENNY. To clap the hands together in the attitude of prayer; part of a rhyme taught to children: 'Clap-a-benny for a penny, one-two-three.' Late 19C. *Yorks.*

CLAP-CANS. A ghost or hobgoblin which makes a clanking

noise as of beating on empty cans. Late 19c. *Yorks.*

CLAPPER. The tongue as used in speaking, especially prattling. Late 19c. *Sussex.*

CLAPPER-BOARD. A wooden contrivance for scaring birds away from crops, consisting of a length of wood on which two smaller pieces are hinged. When shaken it rattles alarmingly. Late 19c. *E. Anglia.*

CLAPPER-CLAW. Chattering or argumentation marked by raised voices, in which a woman or two join to tell a man, usually a husband, a little bit of his own. Also called 'jawbation'. Early 19c.

CLAPPERTIE-CLINK. The sound made by the contrivance in a mill which shakes the hopper so as to make the grain move down to the mill-stones. Early 19c. *Renfrews.*

CLAPPING-TABLE. A table in the kitchen or pantry for chopping and moulding; so called from the sound made by its use. 19c. *E. Anglia.*

CLARISONOUS. Having a clear or shrill sound. 18c.

CLARY. A shrill noise, a ringing cry. Mid 19c. *Shrops.*

CLATCH. The noise caused by the collision of soft bodies; probably of imitative origin. Late 19c. *Scotland.*

CLATTER-BONE. A bone which is supposed to move when one chatters or prates: 'Thy tongue goes like the clatter-bone of a goose's arse'. Early 19c. *Scotland.*

CLATTER-STOUP. A chattering, noisy person; a rattle-pan. Early 19c. *Scotland.*

CLAVICYLINDER. A musical instrument with a keyboard, in which each key causes a rod to press against a revolving glass cylinder. Late 19c.

CLAVVER. A noisy assemblage, especially of crows or hounds. Late 19c. *Yorks.*

CLEASH. The ear, as used for the purposes of unobserved listening or eavesdropping. Early 20c. *Isle of Man.*

CLEIRO. A sharp noise; a shrill sound. Late 19C. *Scotland*.

CLICK-ME-TOAD. A jocular name for a watch, from its ticking. Late 19C. *Lancs*.

CLICK-REEL. A spinner's reel turned by a handle and giving a click when a certain number of threads has been wound. Mid 19C. *Cumber*.

CLICK-UP. A person with a short leg who makes a clicking noise in walking. Late 19C. *Lincs*.

CLICKET. A wooden salt-box with a lid; so called from the noise of its shutting. Late 19C. *Yorks*.

CLICKETING. The noise made by a hasp when the door or gate is shaken by the wind. Late 19C. *Warwicks*.

CLINKERS. Bricks burnt very hard, and not fit to be placed with others; so called from the noise they make when struck. Early 19C. *Hants*.

CLINKSTONE. An igneous rock of feldspathic composition, lamellar in structure, and clinking under the hammer. Late 19C.

CLIT-CLAT. The noise made by a talkative person. Late 19C. *Lancs*.

CLITTER. To make a shrill, rattling noise. 16C.

CLOCHARET. The wheatear, *Saxicola oenanthe*; derived from the Gaelic *cloich*, meaning a stone, and alluding to the resemblance of the bird's cry to a stone being struck. Late 19C. *Angus*.

CLOCKING. The sound made by falling, gurgling water. Late 19C. *Hants*.

CLOCKS. Little black insects, like beetles, which make a ticking noise, often considered a token of death. Mid 19C. *Lincs*.

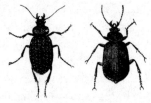

CLOOP. The sound made when a cork is forcibly drawn from a bottle. Mid 19C.

Clowk. To make a gurgling noise, as a liquid when poured from a full bottle. Late 19c. *Banffs.*

Cluck. The noise made by children when going to sleep. Late 19c. *Lincs.*

Cluck-hen. A broody hen that is ready to sit; so called from its agitated clucking. Late 19c. *Surrey.*

Clumput. To stump about noisily. Late 19c. *Berks.*

Clunk. The sound of a liquid coming out of a bottle when the cork has been quickly drawn. 18c. *Scotland.*

Cluntering. The noise made by iron-bound clogs. Early 19c. *N. England.*

Cluther. The sound made by rabbits in their hole, just before they bolt out; to make a noise generally, as by knocking things together. Late 19c. *Kent.*

Coach-trumpet. A horn of about three feet in length and fixed to a coach or other carriage. The wider end passes outside through the roof, whilst the other end is attached to a mouth-piece by a swivel joint. It is of sufficient length to reach the mouth of any person sitting inside the coach, thus allowing them to speak to the coachman or postilion without being obliged to put his head out of the window to give directions. 18c.

Cockathodon. The Manx shearwater, *Puffinus puffinus*; so called in imitation of its hoarse, guttural cry. Mid 19c. *Cornwall and Scilly Isles.*

Cock-bell. An icicle; so called from the faint ringing noise it makes when tapped. 17c. *Kent.*

Cockcrow-route. A route along the shore kept by bargemen, so close to the land as to be within earshot of the cock's crow. Early 20c.

Cocket. The noise made by a pheasant when disturbed. Late 19c. *Surrey.*

Cockieleerie. The noise made by a cock in crowing. Late 19c. *Scotland.*

Cockles. To cry cockles: to be hanged; from the noise made by strangulation. 19C.

Cockling. To make a noise in swallowing. Mid 19C. *Northum.*

Cocky-keeko. The noise made by a cock in crowing. Late 19C. *Cheshire.*

Coffin. When a cinder springs out of the fire it is called either a purse or a coffin; the distinction depending not on the shape, but on its making a crackling noise, or being perfectly silent; in the former case it is called a purse. This idle piece of superstition was originally, no doubt, supposed to forebode wealth or death to the person nearest to whom it first fell. Mid 19C. *Co. Durham.*

Cog. A form of interrupted respiration, in which the interruptions are very even, three or four to each inspiration; as in cogged breath. 19C.

Collan-bing. A ringing sound in the ears. Early 20C. *Isle of Man.*

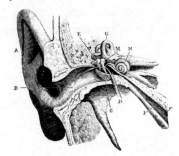

Collery-horn. A long brass horn of shrill note, often used at funerals; sometimes absurdly corrupted to 'cholera-horn'. Late 19C. *Anglo-Indian.*

Colt-pixy. An apparition alleged to neigh to the horses of travellers, with the intent of luring them onto boggy or marshy ground. 19C. *Hants.*

Commingler. A device for noiseless heating of water by steam, in a vessel filled with a porous mass, as of pebbles. 19C.

Complaining. The creaking of a wooden ship at sea. 19C.

Concent. A harmony or concord of sounds; a concert of voices. 16C.

Conk. A large conch-shell of the genus *Strombus*, imported and then fitted with a mouth-piece. In former times it was used by fishermen as a fog-horn, producing as it did a loud and distinctive note on being blown. Late 19C. *Cornwall.*

CONSTANT-SCREAMER. Satirical term for the concertina, which is a machine played by an upward pull, and a downward pressure of the construction, which has much the appearance of a tubular Japanese lantern. Mid 19C. *London.*

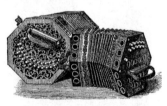

COOEE. A peculiar whistling sound made by the Aborigines as a call or signal, and adopted by shepherds. The final 'e' is a very high note, a sort of prolonged screech, that resounds for miles through the bush, and thus enables parties that have lost each other to ascertain their relative positions. 19C. *Australia.*

COOK. To make the noise of the cuckoo. 17C.

COOPERS. The name given to benevolent sprites which were alleged to make a hammering noise in the cellars of houses. Such an occurrence was said to foretell a catch of pilchards. Late 19C. *Cornwall.*

COOTER. To coo, make the sound of the wood-pigeon. Late 19C. *Gloucs.*

COR. To cry; to call. 19C. *English Gypsy.*

CORONACH. A funeral song or lamentation; a dirge. 18C. *Scotland.*

CORRENOY. A disturbance in the bowels; a rumbling noise in the stomach. Late 19C. *Scotland.*

COTTABUS. A pastime of young men in ancient Greece, consisting of throwing a portion of wine at a metal basin, so as to produce a distinctive sound which was interpreted as an augury.

COW-MOUTHED. Bellowing, loud-voiced, blaring. Late 19C. *Worcs.*

COWOWING. The caw or noise made by rooks. Late 19C. *Hants.*

CRACK. The sound caused by flatulence. 16c.

CRACK-THE-MONICA. To ring the chairman's table-bell in a music hall, so as to inform the audience applauding a singer who had retired that he or she would appear again. Late 19c. *London.*

CRACKEE-CRACKEE. Evangelistic preaching. Maori pidgin from the whalers' slang 'crack', meaning to boast or brag. Early 19c. *New Zealand.*

CRACKIL. The wren, *Troglodytes troglodytes*; so called from its cry, which is surprisingly loud for one so small. Late 19c. *Devon.*

CRAKE. To cry, or utter its note, as the crow or the corncrake does; the carrion crow, *Corvus corvus.* 18c. *Scotland and N. England.*

CRAKY. Of the voice: hoarse and shaky. Late 19c. *Cornwall.*

CRAMBO-SONG. Still heard in the remoter parts of England, a roystering ballad of a cavalier, wine, and women swing. From the Spanish *caramba*, shortened by the omission of the first vowel. Probably brought over by Philip of Spain; or a countess in the suite of Catherine of Braganza, or Charles II may be answerable. Late 19c.

CRAMBROOKOS. A drum. 19c. *English Gypsy.*

CRAMP. The noise made by swine whilst they are eating. Late 19c. *Northants.*

CRANK. The creaking, harsh noise made by an ungreased wheel, &c. Mid 19c. *Scotland and N. England.*

CRANK-BIRD. The lesser-spotted woodpecker, *Dryobates*

minor; so called from its cry resembling the creaking produced by the turning of a windlass. Late 19c. *Gloucs.*

CRAP. To snap, break with a sudden sound; as of anything brittle. Early 19c. *W. England.*

CREAK-WARNER. A watchman's rattle; used, too, of the watchman himself. Late 19c. *Yorks.*

CREAN. To bellow, make a noise like a bull; to bawl, shout. 18c. *N. England.*

CREIST. To make the laboured sound in breathing caused by sitting in a constrained position. Late 19c. *Orkney.*

CREPITATE. To make a series of small, sharp, rapidly repeated explosions or sounds, as salt in fire; to crackle, as of the tissues of the lungs. Mid 19c.

CREPITUS. The noise produced by a sudden discharge of wind from the bowels. Late 19c.

CRIBBING. A vicious habit of a horse; crib-biting. The horse lays hold of the crib or manger with his teeth and draws air into the stomach with a grunting sound. Mid 19c.

CRICK. A sharp noise, as made in the knee-joint when one is kneeling down. Late 19c. *Berks.*

CRICKET-BIRD. The grasshopper warbler, *Locustella naevia*; so called from its cry, which resembles the note of a cricket. Late 19c.

CRINK-TO-CRANK. A rattling sound in which a metallic ring predominates. Late 19c. *Somerset and Hants.*

CROAK. To die; so called from the gurgling sound a person makes when the breath of life is departing. Late 19c.

CROAKER. A small American fish, *Micropogon undulatus*, of the Atlantic coast. When caught these fishes make a croaking sound; whence the name, which is often corrupted into crocus. 18c.

CROAKING-LIZARD. A kind of lizard found commonly around Kingston; so called from the noise it emits. This, and its slow creeping motion, has given it an unsavoury reputation. Early 19c. *Jamaica*.

CROAKUM-SHIRE. A name given to Northumberland and Newcastle, from the croaking pronunciation of the inhabitants. Late 19c. *N. England*.

CRONK. To croak, make the harsh note of a raven or frog; to grumble. 18c. *N. and W. England.*

CROOD. To make the murmuring sound of a dove. Mid 19c. *Scotland*.

CROONER. The grey gurnard, *Trigla gurnardus*; so called from its 'crooning' noise made when caught. 18c. *Scotland*.

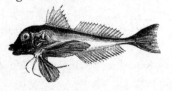

CROOSLE. To make a low whimpering noise, like an infant just waking; to cry, whine. Mid 19c. *Devon*.

CROSE. To whine in sympathy with any person in pain or distress; to speak in a whining, flattering tone of voice. Late 19c. *Scotland*.

CROUPY-CRAW. The raven, *Corvus corax*; so called from its hoarse cry. Late 19c. *N. England*.

CROW-KEEPER. A boy employed to scare crows from new-sown land. Besides lustily whooping, he carries an old gun from which he may crack a little powder, and sometimes puts in a few small stones, but seldom hits. Late 19c. *E. Anglia*.

CROWDER. A fiddler, especially one who plays to an audience. 16c.

CROWDY-CRAWN. A rude musical instrument formed by a skin

stretched on a hoop or over a sieve. Late 19c. *Cornwall*.

CROWDY-KIT. A small fiddle. Early 19c. *Somerset*.

CROWDY-MAIN. An uproarious crowd; a noisy fight arranged for sport between dogs or cockerels. Late 19c. *Northum*.

CROWP. To croak, as toads do; to speak hoarsely; to rumble or murmur, as one's bowels do when full of wind. Late 19c. *Midlands and N. England*.

CRUCKLE. To make a crackling noise, as that produced by the ends of a broken bone rubbing together. Late 19c. *Suffolk*.

CRUMPH. The noise made by the bursting of a shell or bomb. Early 20c.

CRUNE. The subdued bellowing and moaning of a bull; sometimes also applied to the roaring noise

made by a child. Mid 19c. *Co. Durham and Cumber*.

CRY. The louder sound made by the Dartmoor rivers at certain times, said to betoken the arrival of bad weather. Late 19c. *Devon*.

CRYING-THE-NECK. A harvest-time custom in which the last sheaf to be cut is greeted by the labourers with a cheer. 18c.

CRY-UP. The peculiar note or tone of buzzing emitted by bees within the hive, made when they are on the point of swarming. Early 19c. *Cleveland*.

CUCKOLD. The red gurnard, *Trigla cuculus*; so called in allusion to the cuckoo-like note it emits when caught. Early 19c. *Cornwall*.

CUCKOO-FOOT-ALE. A custom among the colliers of Shropshire who, on hearing the first cuckoo of the year, cease their labours for the day and drink ale outdoors to welcome the bird. 19C.

CUDDLIE. A whispering or secret muttering among a number of people. Late 19C. *N. Scotland.*

CUR-DOO. The cooing sounds that doves make at roost. Mid 19C. *Galloway.*

CURMURRING. A rumbling sound, especially that made in the bowels by flatulence. 18C.

CURWILLET. The sanderling, *Calidris alba* ; so called from its short, whistling call-note. Late 19C. *Cornwall.*

CURVEW-BELL. At Blewbury it has been the custom for this to be rung regularly between Michaelmas and Lady Day, and many a time those who have been lost on the adjacent downs have hailed the sound of this bell. 19C. *Oxfords.*

CUT-CEDAR-BOARD. To snore; a jocular allusion to the noise made by sawing cedar logs. Early 20C. *Jamaica.*

CUT-ENGLISH. To speak in a high-flown polysyllabic way, with such devices of awesome verbalism as preachers are wont to use. Late 19C. *Jamaica.*

CUTTERING. Talking in a low, conspiratorial voice. Late 19C. *Yorks.*

CYMBAL-DRUM. An invention by which a performer may obtain a simultaneous effect with the cymbal and drum from a single blow of the drum-stick. The cymbal is fixed inside the drum, so that a blow in the exact centre of the drum-skin presses forward a hammer to sound the cymbal. Mid 19C.

D

DANDO'S-DOGS. The cries of ghostly hounds heard on moorland during stormy nights; so called after a priest who was believed to have been carried off by the Devil for hunting on Sundays. 19c. *Cornwall*.

DARK. To listen with sinister intentions; to eavesdrop; to listen eagerly or take mental notes of what is said with the object of making use of the information obtained. 18c. *Co. Durham, Yorks. and Cumber.*

DARKING-DOG. A man who listens attentively to everything said with great eagerness, but at the same time as if it were a subject of little interest to him. Late 19c. *Co. Durham and Yorks.*

DEAD-BELL. The funeral or death-bell; the sound of ringing in the ears. Late 19c. *Scotland.*

DEAD-CHACK. The tapping sound made by a woodworm in the house, the death-watch. Late 19c. *N. England.*

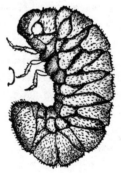

DEAD-DRAP. A drop of water falling intermittently on a floor, with a hollow and leaden sound, thought to be an omen of death. Late 19c. *Banffs.*

DEAD-KNOCK. A loud and mysterious stroke as of a switch

37

upon the door or bed, supposed to announce the death of some relation of the person who hears it. Mid 19C. *Lothian*.

DEAD-RUCKLE. The sound emitted by a dying person. Late 19C. *Lothian and Roxburghs*.

DEATH-COACH. A rumbling sound supposed to betoken death. Late 19C. *Northants*.

DEATH-HUNTER. A running patterer or stationer who announces and sells accounts of all the murders that become topics of public conversation. Mid 19C. *London*.

DEATH-WARNER. The death-watch beetle, *Xestobium rufovillosum*; so called after its ticking noise, which is taken as a sign of impending death. Late 19C. *Yorks*.

DEE-DEE. A deaf mute, or one feigning the affliction. Early 20C. *United States*.

DENTILOQUENT. The quality of speech made through the teeth when the jaws are kept closed. 17C.

DENTIPHONE. A medical instrument which, placed against the teeth, conveys sound to the auditory nerve. 19C.

DERRUM. A deafening noise; a confusion of sounds. Late 19C. *Yorks*.

DEVIL-SCREAMER. The swift, *Apus apus*; so called from its harsh call. Late 19C. *Yorks*.

DEVIL'S-KNELL. The name given to the ringing on Christmas Eve of the tenor bell at All Saints Church in Dewsbury. The bell is rung once for each year since Christ's birth, and is so named from the belief that the Devil died when Christ was born. 19C. *Yorks*.

DHONK. To thump noisily. Late 19c. *Isle of Man.*

DIACOUSTICS. That branch of natural philosophy which treats of the properties of sound as affected by its passing through different mediums; called also diaphonics. 17c.

DICTOGRAPH. A telephonic instrument for office or similar use, having a sound-magnifying device which enables the ordinary mouthpiece to be dispensed with. Early 20c.

DIDDLE. To keep time to music with the feet; a jingle of music, as of a fiddle. Early 19c. *N. England and Scotland.*

DIDO. A great noise. Late 19c. *Cornwall.*

DING-DONG. The call to a meal at a mining or logging camp. Early 20c. *United States.*

DINGER. A system of bells for relaying messages in a military camp or barracks. Early 20c.

DINLING. Vibrating, rattling. Early 19c. *Scotland.*

DIPPURL. The common tern, *Sterna hirundo*; so called in imitation of the bird's cry, which resembles the sound of the word 'pirl'. Late 19c. *Norfolk.*

DIRL. To vibrate noisily, as when sharply struck or shaken, or in response to loud sounds; to produce loud vibrations. Early 19c. *Scotland.*

DOG'S-LETTER. The letter R; so called from its resemblance in sound to the growl of a dog. 18c.

DOODLEBUG. A kind of beetle which is noisy in flight. Early 20c. *United States.*

DOOFF. A dull-sounding fall, like that of a loaded sack coming to the ground. Early 19c. *Scotland.*

DOPPET. To play a musical instrument in a jerky, halting fashion. Late 19c. *Gloucs.*

DORE. To deafen with noise. Late 19c. *Orkney and Shetland.*

DOUDLE. The root of the common reed, *Arundo phragmites*, of which children make a sort of musical instrument similar to the oaten pipe of the ancients. Late 19c. *Roxburghs.*

DOYST. To fall with a heavy sound. Late 19c. *Scotland.*

DRAKE'S-DRUM. A myth of recent origin claiming that the drum of Sir Francis Drake, after its return to England, has been heard beating when invasion threatens, or during other significant events. Early 20c.

DRANE. A drone, usually applied to a wasp. 18c. *W. England.*

DRANE-POKE. A drawling and tiresome speaker. Late 19c. *Yorks.*

DRATE. To drawl, speak in a monotonous or indistinct manner. 18c. *N. England.*

DREAM-HOLE. One of the slits or loopholes left in the walls of steeples and towers to allow the sound of the bells to escape. 16c. *Gloucs. and Yorks.*

DREEN. The gratified sound made by a cow during milking. Late 19c. *Cumber.*

DREEP. A melancholy tone of voice; to speak slowly. Late 19c. *Cumber.*

DREM. The sound of a bell or trumpet. *Middle English.*

DRILSY. A monotonous, continued sound; a low murmuring or hum. Late 19c. *Cornwall.*

DRING. To sing in a slow, melancholy manner; the growing noise of a kettle before it boils. 18c. *Scotland.*

DRIZZEN. To low as a cow or ox, especially to make a subdued and plaintive sound when wanting food. Late 19c. *Scotland and Ireland.*

DRONE. A dull speaker or preacher; the mourning sound

emitted by children when out of humour. Early 19c. *Scotland and Orkney.*

DROOL. To sound or trill in a sad, mournful way; to cry out sadly. Early 19c. *Roxburghs.*

DROW. A melancholy sound, like that of the dashing of waves heard at a distance. Late 19c. *Lothian.*

DRUM. To make the peculiar sound by snipe in the breeding season. Mid 19c. *Lancs.*

DRUMFISH. Any fish of the family *Sciaenidae*, which makes a loud noise by means of its air bladder. 18c.

DRUMMER. A large cockroach, *Blatta gigantea*; so called from its habit of drumming with its head on woodwork as a sexual call. 18c. *Jamaica.*

DULCITONE. An instrument with a keyboard, in which tones are produced by felt-covered hammers striking at an array of steel tuning forks. Late 19c.

DULLOR. A dull, moaning sound; a loud, continuous noise; a row. Late 19c. *E. Anglia.*

DUMB-CAKE. A special cake prepared as a joint effort by several women, following complicated instructions and in complete silence, as a form of love divination. Mid 19c. *N. England.*

DUMBLEDORE. A humble-bee, a large species of wild bee of the genus *Bombus.* The name is evidently expressive of the noise made by this insect. 18c. *Hants. and W. England.*

DUMMY. A locomotive with condensing engines, and, hence, without the noise of escaping steam. Mid 19c. *United States.*

DUNDER. To rumble, give out a loud thundering noise; to knock or strike with a loud noise. Early 19c. *Northum. and Scotland.*

DUNDER-CLUGS. A facetious name for a Dutchman, so called

from the wooden shoes worn by him and the noise they make. Late 19c. *Shetland.*

DUNDERED. Naval term for the condition of being deafened by gunfire, used particularly if a man is stupified by it. Early 20c.

DUNYEL. To jolt, with the idea of its being accompanied with a hollow sound. Late 19c. *Lanarks.*

DUTCH-CONCERT. A discordant noise; a confused babel of sounds, as when several tunes are played together. 18c.

DUTTER. To confound or confuse with noise; to make a loud, disagreeable noise. Mid 19c. *Wilts. and E. Anglia.*

DUVVER. The noise of a crying child. Late 19c. *Essex.*

DYNAMOSCOPY. The auscultation of the sound, consisting of a hollow rumbling, produced by certain muscular contractions in the body. Heard especially on application of the stethoscope to the fingertips. Mid 19c.

DYSPHONIA. A difficulty in producing vocal sounds; enfeebled or depraved voice. 18c.

E

EAR-BELL. A small bell fastened as an adornment to a horse's head-collar. 19C. *E. Anglia*.

EAR-OF-DIONYSIUS. A kind of ear trumpet with a flexible tube; named from the Sicilian tyrant who constructed a device to overhear the prisoners in his dungeons. 19C.

EAR-STRING. A supposed tendon or nerve of the ear, which can be broken from listening to someone or something disagreeable. Early 20C. *United States*.

ECHOMETRY. The art of measuring the duration of sounds or echoes; the art of building vaults to produce echoes. Early 19C.

ECHOSCOPE. An instrument for intensifying sounds produced by percussion of the thorax. Mid 19C.

EGOPHONY. A tremulous resonance heard during auscultation in cases of pleurisy. Early 19C.

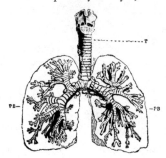

ELECTROPHONE. A means of distributing to subscribers the sounds of theatrical performances and church sermons, via the telephone. Early 20C.

ELF-MILL. A ticking sound in timber, viewed as a warning of death; a sound like that of a mill, heard when listening at a hole in the ground. Late 19C. *Caithness*.

ELLIPTICAL-ECHO. Not strictly speaking an echo, but simply a resonance, inasmuch as the listener does not hear a sound repeated, but merely magnified. All 'whispering galleries' may be classed under this category. Mid 19C.

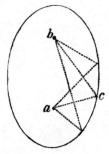

ERTHE-HORN. A contrivance for making a noise underground. *Middle English.*

EUPHONICON. A variety of upright piano. 19C.

EUPHOTINE. A musical instrument consisting of 22 tuning forks, to each of which is secured a thin piece of glass, encompassing three octaves in total. The tone of each fork is drawn out by a moistened finger passing over the glass attached to the tines of the fork. Mid 19C.

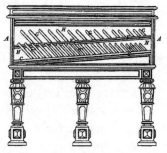

EUTONY. The pleasantness of a word's sound. 19C.

EXALTATION-OF-LARKS. Said by bird-fanciers of several larks when they ascend until out of sight, but not out of hearing. In poetic language larks are spoken of as songstresses, though the male alone sings. Early 19C.

F

Fartynge-grasse. A plant most likely of the genus *Rhinanthus*; so called from the rattling noise of its seeds when ripe. *Middle English.*

Fiddle-father. The bass fiddle. Late 19c. *Yorks.*

Fiddle-grass. The codlins-and-cream, *Epilobium hirsutum*; so called because the stems are by children stripped of their leaves, and scraped across one another fiddle-fashion, so that they make a squeaking sound. Late 19c. *Yorks.*

Fiddler's money. A sixpence; from being the usual sum paid by each couple for music at country wakes and hops. Early 19c.

Fidther. To make a slight rustling sound, as a mouse or rat does among straw, &c. Late 19c. *Worcs.*

Fire-drum. A drum beaten to give an alarm of fire. Late 19c. *Scotland.*

Fist-whistle. In order to make a whistle of the fists, the two thumbs should be placed in juxtaposition; the palm of the right hand being laid over the palm of the left, and the ends of the fingers folded over the backs of the hands. The part contiguous to the two wrists must then be brought together, so as to form a sort of box. By blowing with a smart jerk downwards through the knuckles of the thumb, a whistle may be produced like the barking of a dog. Mid 19c.

FIZGIG. A firework, made of damp powder, which makes a fizzing or hissing noise when it explodes; a child's toy which emits a whirring sound when set in motion. 17c.

FIZMER. To fidget unquietly, perhaps from the rustling noise produced by petty agitations. Late 19c. *E. Anglia.*

FLAW. A sudden burst of noise and disorder. 17c.

FLICKET-A-FLACKET. Onomatopoetic for a noise of flapping and flicking. 19c.

FLOP. The sound that a flat body makes when falling into water. Late 19c. *Lincs.*

FLUCTISONOUS. Sounding or roaring like waves at sea. 17c.

FLUSK. To make a whirring, fluttering sound. Mid 19c. *Lancs. and Yorks.*

FLUTTER-ECHO. An acoustical phenomenon comprised of a series of echoes made in rapid succession and typically occurring between parallel surfaces as with the walls of a school-room, and producing a characteristic metallic or ringing sound. Early 20c.

FOG-WATCH. A ship's watch kept at night in thick weather, with the duty of ringing the upper-deck bell regularly. Early 20c.

FOGS. Railwaymen's term for the miniature detonators carried on every locomotive, and which in emergencies could then be clipped to a rail to warn trains of obstructions ahead. Early 20C.

FOO-FOO. An amateur band of the comb-and-paper variety, raised in the ship's company. Early 20C.

FORTY-LUNGED. Stentorian; given to shouting. Late 19C.

FOTHERING-HORN. A horn sounded to call the farm servants to the 'fothering', or last feeding-time of horses and cattle, in the evening. Late 19C. *Northum.*

FOUR-O'CLOCK. The noisy friarbird, *Philemon corniculatus*; imitative of the sound of one of its calls. Early 20C. *Australia.*

FOURTEEN-HUNDRED. A cry warning that a stranger is in the Stock Exchange. The cry is said to have had its origin in the fact that for a long while the number of members never exceeded 1399; and it was customary to hail every newcomer as the fourteen hundredth. Late 19C. *London.*

FOWL-CROW. The first cock-crow of the morning. Early 20C. *United States.*

FRACCHEN. To make a harsh or strident noise; to creak loudly. *Middle English.*

FRAGOR. A loud and sudden sound; the report of anything bursting; a crash. 17C.

FRANK. The heron, *Ardea cinerea*; so called in imitation of its harsh, abrupt cry. Late 19C. *Suffolk.*

FRAP. A short sharp sound like that of a pop-gun, or the bursting of an inflated paper bag; a primitive kind of firework. Late 19C. *N. England.*

FREAM. The noise made by a boar at rutting-time. 16C.

FREE-AND-EASY. A club held at a low public-house, the members of which meet in the tap room or parlour for the purpose of drinking and hearing each other sing. These gatherings are generally called harmonic meetings by the landlord. Early 19c. *London.*

FRIZZLING. A hissing, sputtering sound as in frying. Early 19c. *Northants. and Devon.*

FRUSH. Noise; clatter; the crash of weapons being broken. *Middle English.*

FUFF. An explosive sound; a splutter; the hissing or 'spitting' sound made by a cat. Early 19c. *Scotland.*

FULMINATING-ALARM. A mechanical arrangement in which caps containing small quantities of fulminating powder are set at the doors of dwelling houses and other buildings. When an entry is attempted, the mechanism is brought into action and causes the percussion of the caps, thereby giving an alarm to the occupants of the house. Its construction makes it possible to be set from the outside of the door when closed. Mid 19c.

FUNG. To emit a sharp, whizzing sound. Late 19c. *Perths.*

FUTHIR. The whizzing sound caused by quick motion. Late 19c. *Aberdeens.*

FUZZ. To fly off in minute particles with a fizzing sound like water from hot iron. 18c.

G

GABBLERATCHET. The nightjar, *Caprimulgus europaeus*; so called from its distinctive call. 18c. *Lancs. and Yorks.*

GABRIEL'S-HOUNDS. A popular name for the noise made by distant curlews or geese, ascribed to damned souls whipped on by the angel Gabriel. 18c. *N. England.*

GAFF. To laugh loudly. Early 19c. *Scotland.*

GALDER. To prate in a noisy and vulgar manner. Late 19C. *E. Anglia.*

GALEE. Loud, foul-mouthed and vituperative abuse. Late 19C. *Anglo-Indian.*

GALLAFER. A prattling sound; a loud noise; a burst of laughter. Late 19C. *Shetland.*

GALLEY-BIRD. The green woodpecker, *Picus viridis*; so called from its loud, laughing note. From the Anglo-Saxon *gal*, meaning merry. Late 19C. *Sussex.*

GAMUT. The musical scale; so called from the Greek *gamma*, which marked the last of the series of notes in musical notation, and the Latin *ut*, from the old hymn to St John which begins 'Ut queant laxis', used in singing the scale. 15C.

GARM. To scold, vociferate loudly; to speak in an impudent, harsh voice. Late 19C. *Cornwall.*

GAS-GUN. A signalling device in which sound is produced by the explosion of gas in a pipe, used to give guidance to shipping in conditions of poor visibility. Mid 19C.

GAS-WHISTLE. A whistle for signalling on the railways, whereby it is sounded by the application of hydrogen gas and carbonic acid gas with an admixture of atmospheric air. Mid 19C.

GASTROMANCY. Divination by interpreting sounds from the stomach or bowels. Late 19C.

GAUNER. To bark; to scold with a loud voice. Late 19C. *Clydes.*

GAW-HAW. To talk or shout loudly. Late 19C. *Scotland.*

GAWK. Of heavy soils: to emit a groaning sound or 'squelch' when dug. Late 19C. *Gloucs.*

GAWTHRUSH. The misselthrush, *Turdus viscivorus*; so called in imitation of its harsh note. Late 19C. *Northants.*

GECKEN. To mock with loud and silly laughter; to laugh like a fool. Mid 19C. *Yorks.*

GECKO. A kind of house lizard; so called as an onomatopoeia from the creature's reiterated 'chuck, chuck, chuck' utterance. Late 19C. *Anglo-Indian.*

GEOPHONE. A listening instrument invented by the French to detect enemy sapping and underground mining operations. Early 20C.

GEWGAW. A trump or mouthorgan. Mid 19C. *Scotland and N. England.*

GIBBERWOLING. Yowling or

caterwauling; from 'gib', an old male cat. Late 19c. *Gloucs.*

GIG. To creak; to move so as to produce a creaking noise. 18c. *Yorks. and Lincs.*

GIGGER. A tailor's sewing machine; so called from the noise of its operation. Late 19c.

GIGGLES-NEST. As in, 'Have you found a giggles-nest?' Asked of one tittering, or else given to immoderate or senseless laughter. 19c.

GILL, GIV. To sing. 19c. *English Gypsy.*

GILLY, GIVELLY. A song. 19c. *English Gypsy.*

GILLYAWS. Printed songs or ballads. 19c. *English Gypsy.*

GIN-AND-FOG. A peculiar hoarseness of the voice, generally believed to be caused by the abuse of alcohol. Late 19c. *Theatrical slang.*

GITBOX. The guitar. Early 20c. *United States.*

GITTERN. A musical instrument stringed with gut and played by plucking, the predecessor of the guitar. 16c.

GIZZENED. When a person's throat rattles from strangulation, it is said to be 'gizzened'. Late 19c. *Yorks.*

GLAFTER. A burst of laughter. Late 19c. *Orkney and Shetland.*

GLAG. To make a noise in the throat as though choking. Late 19c. *Banffs.*

GLASS-HARMONICA. An instrument invented by Franklin, the sounds of which were produced from bell-shaped glasses placed on a framework that revolved at its centre, while the rims were touched by the moistened finger. 18c.

GLAVER. A loud and confused noise; clamour, din. *Middle English.*

GLEANING-BELL. In former times, the bell which was rung in the morning as notice to begin gleaning or collecting leftover crops from the fields. 19C. *Essex.*

GLINK. The sound which a liquid makes in escaping from a narrow-mouthed vessel. Late 19C. *Northants.*

GLOAR. To bawl, to howl; to make a coarse sound. Late 19C. Isle of Man.

GLOUK. The sound made by a crow. Late 19C. *Galloway.*

GLOX. Of liquids: to roll about, make a gurgling sound when shaken inside a vessel. Mid 19C. *Wilts. and Hants.*

GLUCK. A gurgling sound, as made by lifting the feet from a mire. Late 19C. *Forfar.*

GLUDDER. The sound caused by a fall in mire or slush. Early 19C. *Ayrshire.*

GLUMSH. To swallow food noisily. Late 19C. *Caithness.*

GNAR. To snarl or growl. 16C.

GOBBLE. A deep, thick, resonant voice; noisy talk. Late 19C. *E. Anglia.*

GODLI. Noise, disturbance. 19C. *English Gypsy.*

GOILBRUL. Of a cow: to give a loud, prolonged lowing sound. Late 19C. *Shetland and Orkney.*

GOLDER. To shout; to speak or hail boisterously or with menace. Early 19C. *Northum., Cumber. and Scotland.*

GOLLAR. To emit a gurgling sound; to utter loud but inarticulate sounds. Late 19C. *Scotland.*

GORGE. To make a gurgling 'squelching' sound; the noise

made when the shoes are filled with water. Late 19c. *Fife*.

GOSHORN. A horn used for calling geese; an obnoxious noise, clamour. *Middle English*.

GOSLING-PATCH. The period in which a boy's voice is changing. Late 19c. *United States*.

GOUL, GOWL. Of the wind: to blow fitfully with a hollow sound. Late 19c. *N. England*.

GOW. A crowd of men engaged in close conversation; a place where such talk tends to occur. Late 19c. *Cornwall*.

GRAIG. To utter an inarticulate sound of contempt. Late 19c. *Banffs. and Aberdeens*.

GRAND-CLAVILYRA. A kind of keyed harp, where the strings may be struck at or near the middle by playing upon the keys in the same manner as on a pianoforte. This is principally effected by giving a revolving motion to a plectrum

and causing it, when forced by the key, to strike the string as it advances in its orbit. Early 19c.

GRAVISONOUS. Having a deep or heavy sound. 18c.

GREET. To cry, to wail piteously. 17c. *Scotland and N. England*.

GREETING. The process of a *Cumina* cult marriage ceremony whereby the various gods and zombies are summoned by vigorous drumming to inhabit the drums themselves. Their presence is indicated by an increase in the tempo of the rhythmic beating on the rim of the drum. Early 20c. *Jamaica*.

GRIDDLE. To sing hymns in the street as a preliminary to begging. Early 20c. *United States*.

GRIDDLER. A person who sings in the streets from memory without a printed copy of the words. 19c. *London*.

GRIDE. To cut with a grating sound. Early 19c.

GRILL. To snarl or snap as a dog. Early 19c. *Suffolk and Devon*.

GRIN. To strike on plates with knives and forks, beat with the feet, and shout at the top of the voice, in an effort to make the victim grin. Late 19c.

GRIND. To shout the praises of a circus or a show in an effort to draw patronage; the shouting that is so done. Early 20c. *United States.*

GRINDER. The restless fly-catcher, *Seisura inquieta*. It makes a noise like a scissors grinder, to which the name alludes. Early 20c. *Australia.*

GRISBATING. Chattering or grinding of the teeth. *Middle English.*

GRIZZLE. To whimper; to complain. Late 19c. *Essex.*

GROANING. Parturition; the time at which a woman is in labour. A 'groaning-cake', a kind of rich fruitcake, may be prepared for a woman recovering from the effort of childbirth, or else made by her during the early stages of labour as a distraction. 18c.

GROONGE. To grunt like a pig; to growl, grumble, murmur. 18c. *Northum.*

GROPING-FOR-JESUS. Public prayer; derived from one of the imitative military orders of Booth, the creator of the Salvation Army. They used the cry 'Grope for Jesus, grope for Jesus', when the followers fell upon their knees. Late 19c.

GROSS. Gruff, deep-sounding. Late 19c. *Kent.*

GROUT-HEADED. Said of one who is thoughtlessly noisy. Late 19c. *Sussex.*

GROWLER. An abundant fish of the perch family, *Grystes salmonoides*; so called from the sound it emits when caught. Late 19c. *United States.*

GROWZE. To eat in a noisy manner; to crunch. Late 19c. *Notts. and Lincs.*

GROZER-SQUEALS. The outcry of itinerant vendors of gooseberries. Late 19c. *Northum.*

GRUCCHINGE. Murmuring, grumbling; growling of animals; rumbling in the stomach or bowels. *Middle English.*

GRUFFLE. To make a sort of growling noise in the throat, as

men are wont to do in sleep or in drink. Late 19c. *E. Anglia.*

GRUMPHER. To clear the voice. Late 19c. *Northum.*

GRUNE. The noise made by a pig. Mid 19c. *Co. Durham.*

GRUNT. Certain food fishes, especially of the genus *Haemulon*; so called from the grunting noise they make when caught. Individual species are identified as the black-tail grunt, the red-mouth grunt, &c. 18c. *Jamaica.*

GRUNTER. The wireless spark-gap transmitter on board a ship; so called from the abrupt and repeated buzzing sound produced by the electric spark during its operation. Early 20c.

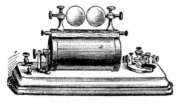

GRUNTLE. To grunt in a low key; to groan slightly; to grumble, complain. Early 19c.

GRUZZLE. To speak huskily; to make a faint inarticulate sound. Late 19c. *Lothian and Renfrews.*

GUBBLE. To make a thick, inarticulate sound, as of a viscous liquid or indistinct speech. Early 20c.

GUE. A musical instrument; a kind of violin, but having only two strings of horse-hair. Early 19c. *Shetland.*

GUGGLE. The windpipe of a goose, dried and formed into a ring, then filled with lead shot to make a rattle. Late 19c. *Staffs. and Warwicks.*

GUMBI-MAN. A drum player who provides the music for the John Canoe dances held during the Christmas holidays. The drum used is played either with the hand or with a stick, and consists of a small square wooden frame over which a goat-skin is held taut. 18c. *Jamaica.*

GUM-GUM. A musical instrument consisting in hollow iron bowls of various sizes and tones, upon which a man strikes with an iron or wooden stick, not unlike a set of bells; also, the sound so produced. 19C. *Anglo-Indian*.

GUPP. The sound of vomiting. Late 19C. *Shetland and Orkney*.

GURDS. Loud eructations. Late 19C. *Somerset*.

GURGULACIOUN. The gurgling sound emitted by the stomach or bowels. *Middle English*.

GURL. To hurtle with a moaning or howling sound, as the wind does during a storm. Late 19C. *Northum*.

GURRAGH. Clucking; hoarse of voice like a clucking fowl. Early 20C. *Isle of Man*.

GUZZUM. Chatter, noise. Late 19C.

H

HACKER. To hesitate in speech; to stammer, stutter. Late 19C. *N. England.*

HACKLE. To rattle, re-echo. Late 19C. *Wilts.*

HAFFER. To make a noise like the bursting of a pod. Mid 19C. *Somerset.*

HALF-A-PINT-OF-MILD-AND-BITTER. Intimated by a whistled phrase, well known to bar tenders, and quite as readily accepted as a spoken order throughout London, except the West district. Late 19C.

HALLYOCH. A strange gabbling noise, especially that heard when listening to a strange tongue. Early 19C. *Scotland.*

HALSENING. Sounding harshly in the throat; inharmonious; rough. 19C.

HAMMER-AND-TONGS. The noise made by a trotting horse when it strikes the hind shoe against the fore shoe. Late 19C. *Cheshire.*

HAMMERGAG. A boisterous noise. Late 19C. *Suffolk.*

HAN. The sound made by men while cutting wood; the groan or sigh-like voice with which wood-cleavers keep time to their strokes. Mid 19C. *Yorks.*

HANYADU. A call to a bird to come and pick up food thrown to it from a boat. Late 19C. *Shetland and Orkney.*

HAPPEN. To rattle, make a sharp cracking sound. Late 19C. *Somerset.*

HARKER. A listener; still used in the proverb 'Harkers never heard a gude word of themselves'. Late 19C. *Scotland.*

HARMONIC-ECHO. An echo which repeats the original sound in a different tone, pitch or key. Mid 19C.

HARMONOMETER. An instrument for measuring the harmonic relations between sounds. Early 19C.

HARMONY. Uproar, noise, disturbance. Late 19C. *Suffolk.*

HARRY'S-WORRIER. A concertina; so called from 'Harry' being the supposed name of a male costermonger. Late 19C. *London.*

HARVEST-HORN. A tin instrument, blown with dismal sound at harvest-time. Late 19C. *Essex.*

HASK. To emit a hoarse, dry cough; to clear the throat; to make a noise as a dog does when anything sticks in its throat. 18C. *N. England and Scotland.*

HASSLE. To pant; to breathe noisily. Late 19C. *United States.*

HAVEN-SCREAMERS. Nautical name for seagulls, from their wheeling and screaming about the harbour. Early 20C.

HAWCH. To make a loud noise with the lips or mouth in eating. 18C. *W. England.*

HAZEN. To speak sharply; to scold or upbraid. Early 19C. *Gloucs. and Wilts.*

HEAR. To sound; as 'it hears nicely', said of a musical instrument. Late 19C. *Yorks.*

HEARING-CHEAT. The ear; literally, a 'hearing thing'. Late 19C. *Polari.*

HEARTH-SONG. The merry stridulation of the house-cricket, *Acheta domesticus*; produced by the attrition of the anterior pair of wings against each other. 19C.

HEATHER-BLEAT. The snipe, *Gallinago gallinago*; so called from its peculiar drumming noise, caused by the rapid action of the wings when making a downward stoop. Its loud cries were once believed to foretell ill-fortune. Early 19C. *Scotland.*

HEATHER-PEEP. The common sandpiper, *Tringoides hypoleucus*; so called from its plaintive note. Late 19C. *Ayrshire.*

HECK. To make a noise with one's throat. Late 19C. *Norfolk.*

HEDGE-ACCENTOR. The hedge sparrow, *Prunella modularis*; so called from there being a *precentor* to lead a choir, and sometimes a *succentor* to follow, making the bird an *accentor* by adding its simple twittering notes to the great chorus of Nature. Late 19C. *E. Anglia.*

HEDGE-CREEP. A party of youths will decide amongst themselves to 'hedge-creep' a certain couple; that is, follow two lovers along the walks which they frequent, but on the other side of the hedge, or wall, for the purpose of listening to their conversation. Late 19C. *Yorks.*

HEEMLIN. Applied to a continual, rumbling sound. Late 19C. *Banffs.*

HEEZE. A disease of pigs, accompanied with thick breathing and wheezing. Late 19C. *Yorks.*

HERRING-PIECE. A rushing sound in the air caused by the flight of the redwing, *Turdus iliacus*; considered a good omen of fishing. Late 19C. *Kent.*

HEUEN. To make a loud noise as in shouting; of a huntsman: to give a signal by hallowing. *Middle English.*

HEWER. A watchman who occupies a post on high ground to give fishermen warning of the approach of schools of pilchard. He then directs the fishing boats by means of a speaking-trumpet. Late 19C. *Cornwall.*

HEWGAG. A child's toy instrument, consisting of a wooden

tube with a hole near one end, and the other closed by a piece of parchment, the vibration of which produces a harsh wailing sound. Mid 19c.

HICKET. To hiccup, gasp for breath, make a choking sound; to retch. Late 19c. *Kent and Surrey.*

HICK-HAW. To make a piteous noise; the braying of an ass. Late 19c. *Yorks.*

HICK-WALL. The green woodpecker, *Picus viridis*; so called from its loud, laughing call. Late 19c. *Gloucs.*

HI-DIDDLE-DIDDLE. Rhyming slang: a fiddle, meaning a musical instrument. Early 20c. *London.*

HI-HOW. The cow-parsley, *Anthriscus sylvestris*; so called from the sound of a child's instrument made of its stem. Late 19c. *N. Ireland.*

HINCHINARFER. A gruff-voiced woman. Late 19c. *London.*

HIRDY-GIRDY. A disorderly noise, a disturbance. Early 19c. *Northum. and Scotland.*

HIREN. A peculiar sound like wind heard when the air is still, and which is believed to herald the onset of a storm. Late 19c. *W. England.*

HIRRIENT. A high-pitched or trilled sound of speech. Early 19c.

HIRSLE. To move forward with a slight rustling or grating sound. Early 19c. *Scotland.*

HISH. To make a hissing noise to urge a dog forward; to drive away an animal by making a hissing sound. Mid 19c. *Norfolk and Warwicks.*

HISK. To draw the breath through the closed teeth, making a hissing noise. A sign of alarm or fear. 18c. *Cumber. and Westmor.*

HISSER. A frying pan; so called in imitation of the sound made in cooking. Late 19c. *Norfolk.*

HISSING-OWL. The barn owl, *Tyto alba*; from its prolonged hiss made in the daytime. Late 19c.

HIVING-SOUGH. A sound made

by bees before they hive, consisting of a continued buzzing hum full of melancholy-like cadences. Early 19C. *Galloway*.

HOBBING. Holloaing, whooping; making a noise. Late 19C. *Herefs*.

HOBBLE. A coarsely loud laugh. Late 19C. *Dorset*.

HOBSON-JOBSON. A native festal excitement, so called as an Anglo-Saxon rendering of the cries of the Mahommedans as they beat their breasts in the procession of the Moharram: 'Ya Hassan! Yo Hosain!' Late 19C. *Anglo-Indian*.

HOBSON'S-CHOICE. Rhyming slang for the voice. Chiefly used in the acting profession. Late 19C.

HOCKSING. Making a noise deliberately and impertinently in walking; to clatter the feet noisily. Late 19C. *Oxfords., Wilts. and Berks*.

HOCUS-POCUS. Gypsy words of magic. Possibly from *habeas cor-*

pus, which the gypsies pronounce 'hawcus paccus'; else it may be a burlesque rendering of the words of the Roman Catholic service at the delivery of the host, *Hoc est Corpus*, which the early Protestants considered as a species of conjuring, and ridiculed accordingly. 17C.

HODENING, HOODENING. The name once given to a mumming or masquerade on Christmas Eve, still applied to the singing of carols. Mid 19C. *Kent*.

HOG. To snore, the noise made by some persons in snoring, being not much unlike the notes of that animal; by extension, 'to come from Hog's Norton', also meaning to snore. Late 19C. *Leics*.

HOIN. To whine, complain, moan. Late 19C. *Lincs*.

HOLLA-BALUTE. A shouting or cheering. Late 19C. *Devon*.

HOLSTER. To make a noise or racket. 18C. *Devon*.

HOMANY. Noise, disturbance. Late 19C. *Somerset*.

HOME-SCREECH. The misselthrush, *Turdus viscivorus*. Late 19C. *Dorset and Somerset*.

HONK. Naval slang meaning to drink in an impressive way, echoic of the noise that eventually results. Early 20c.

Hooch. An exclamation of joy; a shout, especially one used in the dancing of a reel. Mid 19c. *Scotland.*

Hooi. The sound made by the wind whistling round a corner or through a keyhole. Late 19c. *W. England.*

Hoolybuss. A noise, tumult, disorder. Late 19c. *Cornwall.*

Hoo-roo. A hubbub, noise, tumult. Mid 19c. *N. England.*

Hoost. A rough cough, especially one peculiar to cattle. With the latter it is caused by the presence of worms in the windpipe and bronchial tubes. Late 19c. *W. England and Shrops.*

Hooter. A steam-whistle; a wooden trumpet, so contrived as to make a horrible noise. Late 19c.

Hooting. The noise made by a wheel which requires greasing, when in motion. Late 19c. *Worcs.*

Hoozle. To breathe with a laboured, wheezing noise as when

out of breath. Mid 19c. *Scotland.*

Horse-buss. A loud-sounding kiss or bite. Late 19c.

Horn. The sound of breaking wind. *Middle English.*

Horney. A nose, especially one that resounds in expectoration. Early 19c.

Horn-fair. Rough music made with frying pans, horns, &c., typically reserved for persons whose matrimonial difficulties have attracted the attention of their neighbours. 17c. *Sussex.*

Horse's-leg. A bassoon. An essential instrument in village churches when two or three instrumentalists were responsible for leading the church music before organs became general. Mid 19c. *N. England.*

Horrisonous. Having a terrifying or dreadful sound; making such a sound. 17c.

Hottle. The bubbling sound of anything boiling. Late 19c. *Renfrews.*

Howch. Of the voice: hollow, deep, low, guttural. Late 19c. *N. England and Scotland.*

Howk-chowk. To make a noise as if poking among deep mud. Late 19c. *Scotland.*

HOWLAA. An apparition which wails on the shore before a storm. Early 20C. *Isle of Man.*

HOWLERS. Boys who in former times went round wassailing the orchards. The custom used to be observed on the eve of Epiphany. Mid 19C. *Sussex.*

HSUAN. A curious wind instrument of the ancient Chinese, made of baked clay and with five finger-holes, three of which were placed on one side and two on the opposite side. Its tone was in conformity with the pentatonic scale. Mid 19C.

HUBBADALION. A noise, disturbance. Late 19C. *Cornwall.*

HUBBLE-BUBBLE. A confused noise made by a talkative person, who speaks so quickly that it is difficult to understand what he says or means. 18C.

HUDDY-CRAW. The carrion crow, *Corvus corone*; so called from its hoarse cry. Late 19C. *S. Scotland.*

HUFFLE. A wailing or hollow sound of the wind. Late 19C. *W. England.*

HULDER. A deafening noise or din. Late 19C. *Devon.*

HUMBERING. Humming, buzzing. Late 19C. *Warwicks.*

HUM-BOX. A pulpit, indicative of frequent hesitations of speech. Late 19C.

HUMBUZZ. The cockchafer, *Melolontha melolontha*; so called from the loud, clattering noise it makes whilst in flight, Also, a piece of wood shaped so as to make a humming sound when swung around vigorously on a string. Late 19C. *W. England.*

HUMDRUM. A small low three-wheeled cart, drawn usually by one horse; used occasionally in agriculture. From the peculiarity of its construction, it makes a kind of loud humming noise when it is drawn along. Early 19C. *Somerset.*

HUMDURGEON. Needless noise, commotion. Early 19C.

HUMMER. To hum, murmur; to make a low, rumbling noise; to make a soft lowing noise, as cow does when she sees her calf. 18C. *N. England and E. Anglia.*

HUMMUMS. The name given to two taverns in Covent Garden, each with superior accommodation; so called from the 'hum' of many voices in those premises. Early 19C. *London.*

HUMORIC. Of a sound heard in the stomach or intestines produced by percussion or auscultation with a stethoscope, indicating the presence of both liquid and gas. Early 19C.

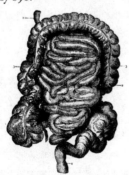

HUMSTRUM. A rude kind of musical instrument; a homemade fiddle fashioned from a mopstick, a bladder or tin canister, and some packthread. Early 19C. *S. and W. England.*

HURKLIN. The peculiar sound made in breathing when there is phlegm in the throat or breast. Late 19C. *Shetland and Orkney.*

HURL. The noise called by the violent fall of any hard material, or the passage of one hard substance over the surface of another. Late 19C. *Caithness and Banffs.*

HURLESS, HURRALESS. Deafened with noise. Late 19C. *Shetland and Orkney.*

HURLIE-GO-THOROW. A noisy disturbance, a racket. Late 19C. *Berwicks.*

HURRAH-BOAT. A paddle-boat with trippers visiting the Fleet at anchor during a Navy Week. The passengers usually cheer wildly as they approach the ships. Late 19C.

HURREN. Of insects: to make a low humming sound; a buzz. *Middle English.*

HUSH. A low, indistinct sound as of breaking waves heard at a distance. Late 19C. *Shetland.*

HUSHEE-BOW. A lullaby. Late 19C. *Isle of Man.*

HUSK. To cough; the sound of coughing; a throat-disease of cattle. Early 19C. *Essex.*

HUSSLE. To wheeze; breathe roughly. Late 19C. *Kent.*

HUZZ. To buzz, hum; to make a whirring noise. Early 19C. *N. England.*

HUZZER. The grasshopper-warbler, *Locustella naevia*; so called from its whirring note. Late 19C. *Lancs.*

HYDATISM. The sound caused by the fluctuation of pus in an abscess. 18C.

HYKE. A cry of encouragement made to dogs during the chase; calling out at or after any one. Early 19C.

HYSTE. A call; an audible signal. Late 19C. *Kent.*

I

INTERJANGLE. To make a dissonant, discordant noise one with another; to talk or chatter noisily. 17C.

INVISIBLE-GIRL. An illusion, the visible part of which consists of a glass or metal globe suspended above one or several speaking-trumpets. The disembodied voice of a girl issues from the trumpets to engage onlookers in conversation and to pass comment upon their appearance. The girl will be hidden in a closet equipped with viewing-mirrors and a speaking-tube. Early 19C. *London*.

IRONSMITH. An East Indian barbet, *Megalaima faber*, inhabiting the Island of Hainan; so called from its insistent note, which resembles the sounds made by a smith. Late 19C.

J

JACK-SQUEALER. The swift, *Apus apus*; so called from its harsh, unmusical scream. Late 19C. *Shrops.*

JAFFSE. To make a noise with the jaws in eating. From Old Norse *kjaptr*, the jaw. Late 19C. *Shetland and Orkney.*

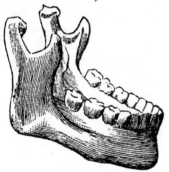

JANKERS. Military slang for punishment of any kind, derived from the underworld term 'janglers', in reference to the jangling of fetters and chains in prison. Early 20C.

JAR-BIRD. The goat-sucker or night-jar, *Caprimulgus europaeus*; so called from its jarring call. Late 19C. *Hants.*

JAR-FLY. A large homopterous insect of the family *Cicadidae*; so called from the shrill sound it produces, likened to a watchman's rattle. Late 19C. *United States.*

JAR-PEG. The green woodpecker, *Picus viridis*; so called from the noise it makes by striking its beak on an old oaken stump, and which is heard in the stillness of the evening for a considerable distance around. Late 19C. *Northants.*

JARGLE. To emit a harsh or discordant sound. 16C.

JAUP. To make a sound like

water shaken in a vessel; figuratively, senseless talk. Early 19C. *Yorks. and Lincs.*

JAWBONE. An instrument formed from the jawbone of an animal, typically a horse, with the teeth loose in the sockets, over which a stick is rattled to make a macabre music. 18C. *Jamaica.*

JENKOVING. A curious instrument for producing resonant tones, consisting of two jars over the mouths of which the player's hands are clapped in quick succession. 18C. *Jamaica.*

JERCOCK. The missel-thrush, *Turdus viscivorus*; so called from the harsh note it utters when alarmed. Late 19C. *Westmor.*

JIBB. The tongue, as used in speech. 19C. *English Gypsy.*

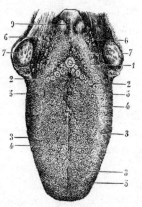

JEYK. To creak, to squeak. Late 19C. *Cumber.*

JILL-HOOTER. An owl, especially the barn-owl, *Strix flammea*; an old man or woman given to grumbling. Mid 19C. *Suffolk.*

JIMMER. To make a disagreeable noise on a fiddle or violin. Early 19C. *Roxburghs.*

JINGLE. Money, especially in small coins; so called from their sound. Early 20C. *Australia.*

JINGLE-BOX. A leathern jack tipped with silver, and hung with bells, once favoured by drunkards as an amusement. Early 19C.

JINGLET. A ball serving as the clapper of a sleigh-bell. Late 19C.

JINGLING-JOHNNIE. A hurdy-gurdy. Mid 19C. *Yorks.*

JINGLING-MATCH. A game set in a large roped ring, into which are introduced a dozen blindfolded men. Another man joins them, without a blindfold but with a bell hung round his neck and his two hands tied behind him. Every time he moves, the bell must ring, as he has no hand to hold it, and so the dozen blind-folded men have to catch him. Mid 19C. *Berks.*

JINK. To jingle. Late 19C. *Essex.*

JOANNA. Rhyming slang for a piano. Early 20C. *London.*

JOGGERING-OMEY. A musician; from Italian *giocar*, to play, and *uomo*, a man. Late 19C. *Theatrical slang.*

JOHNNY-HO. A bird of an un-certain species, but possibly the clapper-rail *Rallus longirostris*; so called for its cry which consists of three distinct articulations. Mid 19C. *Jamaica.*

JOOK. A roadhouse equipped with a coin phonograph or nickel-odeon and space for dancing. Early 20C. *United States.*

JORG. The sound made by shoes when full of water. Late 19C. *Perths.*

JORGLE. The muffled grating noise from broken bones. Early 19C. *Galloway.*

JORINKER. A bird of the tit-mouse species; so called in imitation of its cry. Early 19C. *Galloway.*

JORRAM. A boat-song intended to regulate the strokes of the oars; a song in chorus. Early 19C. *Scotland.*

Jow. To ring or toll a bell; a single strike or pull in the ringing of a bell; the sound of a bell. Early 19C. *Scotland.*

JOWL. To strike the wall of a coal-pit by way of signal or to ascertain from the sound produced the thickness of the wall. Late 19C. *Co. Durham*.

JOWLING. The cracking, rending sound heard when the props are removed from a mine-working. Late 19C. *Northum*.

JUG. To utter a sound resembling this word, as certain birds do, especially the nightingale. 17C.

JUKE. The sound or call emitted by the partridge, *Perdix perdix*; usually made in the morning or at roosting-time in the evening. 17C.

JULK. To produce a sound like liquor shaken in a cask which is

not quite full. Late 19C. *E. Anglia*.

JUMM. The hollow, moaning sound made by the sea in a storm. Early 19C. *Galloway*.

JURR. The noise made by a cascade descending among stones and gravel. Early 19C. *Galloway*.

K

KAE. A caw; the sound made by a jackdaw. Mid 19C. *Banffs.*

KALEIDOPHONE. An instrument consisting of a rod or thin plate with a knob at the end, for showing the curves corresponding with the musical notes produced by the vibrations. Early 19C.

KECK. The noise made in the gullet by sickness; a sound between a cough and a choke. Late 19C. *Yorks. and Lincs.*

KEELIE. The kestrel, *Falco tinnuculus*; so called from its loud, shrill cry. Late 19C. *Lothian.*

KEEPEN. The burden or refrain of a song. Late 19C. *Dorset.*

KEEPING-DOVERCOURT. The making of a great noise; so called from the village of Dovercourt, once celebrated for its scolds, or else the term may come from the great noise made by a local insect called the Dovercourt beetle. Mid 19C. *Essex.*

KERRY. A loud noise, din, disturbance; an outcry, clamorous inquiry. Late 19C. *Cheshire and Shrops.*

KEVEL. A sound like the blow of a hammer; to make such a sound. Early 19C. *N. England.*

KILLARNEY-ECHO. A celebrated echo at the lake of Killarney in Ireland, which renders an excellent second to any simple air played on a bugle. Mid 19C.

Kingle-kangle. Loud, confused, and ill-natured talk. Late 19C. *Fife.*

Kink. To laugh immoderately or loudly; to choke with laughter. Mid 19C. *N. England.*

Kinkin-coff. The whooping-cough. Late 19C. *Yorks.*

Kittle-up. Of a musical instrument: to play, strike up; to tune up. Mid 19C. *Scotland and N. England.*

Klaag. To cackle as a hen does after she has laid her egg; a confused noise of voices. Late 19C. *Shetland.*

Kling-kling. A species of grackle with a sharp, straight beak; so called in imitation of its note, which is something like the creaking of an inn-keeper's sign in a high wind. 18C. *Jamaica.*

Klurmose. The noise of uproar at a distance. Late 19C. *Shetland.*

Knabbler. A person who talks much to no purpose. Mid 19C. *Sussex.*

Knack. To make a sharp clicking sound; to crack, snap, break. 18C. *Scotland and N. England.*

Knack-and-rattle. A quick and noisy mode of dancing with the heels. Late 19C. *N. England.*

Knackers. Castanets made of bone or wood charred at the ends, and with which children beat time. Late 19C. *Yorks. and Northum.*

Knirk. A creaking sound. Late 19C. *Shetland and Orkney.*

Knock. A peculiar thumping noise made by an oil engine which denotes that something is wrong, typically caused by water in the cylinder or loose bearings. Early 20C.

Knockers. Spirits or cobbolds said to haunt mines and which are heard working away on the remote parts of a lode, repeating the blows of the miner's pick or sledge with great precision. Late 19C. *Cornwall and N. Wales.*

Knocker-up. A person, typically an old man or woman, employed to waken factory hands in the morning by tapping on their doors with a long pole, or by blowing dried peas at their windows with a pea-shooter. 19C.

KNOIT. The sound of a heavy stroke or fall. Late 19C. *Scotland*.

KNUCKER. To neigh or whinny. Late 19C. *Sussex, Kent and Surrey*.

KNULLER. A chimney-sweep; so called from the former habit of soliciting jobs by ringing a bell. 19C.

KRED. A weak cough; a grunt. Late 19C. *Isle of Man*.

KREKS. To make a noise in clearing the throat. Late 19C. *Shetland*.

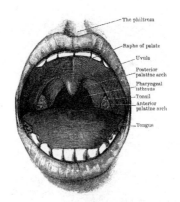

KREEST. A falsetto voice; a forced cry, a groan. Late 19C. *Orkney*.

KROYTL. A bubbling noise like pouring fluid into a bottle. Late 19C. *Shetland*.

L

LABB. The sound of the lapping of waves. Early 19C. *Galloway*.

LAIST. To listen. Late 19C. *Suffolk*.

LAISTLY. A condition of the atmosphere when sounds are heard distinctly; for example, a room in which sounds from without are very easily heard, is a 'laistly' room. Late 19C. *Suffolk*.

LALLATION. An imperfect pro-nunciation of the letter 'r', which the sound of 'l' is substituted for it; a childish utterance. 17C.

LALLING. Loud singing; the emotional singing of certain religious sects. Mid 19C. *Yorks*.

LAMB. The common snipe, *Gallinago gallinago*; so called from the peculiar sound it makes, similar to the bleating of lambs. Late 19C. *Norfolk*.

LAP-CLAP. A loud kiss. Late 19C. *Devon*.

LARRY. A confused noise, as of a number of people all talking together. Late 19C. *Dorset*.

LARYNGOPHONY. The sound of the voice as heard through a stethoscope when the latter is placed upon the larynx. Mid 19C.

LATITAT. A noise, a scolding; idle talk. Early 19C. *Somerset and Shrops*.

LAUGHING-JACK. The kooka-burra, of the genus *Dacelo*; so called from the cackling sound of its cry. Early 20C. *Australia.*

LEDDEN. A noise, a din. 18C. *N. England.*

LEDEN. Birdsong; the cry of a bird. *Middle English.*

LEGE-BELL. The bell carried and sounded before a corpse in procession. *Middle English.*

LERRY. A jingling rhyme spoken by mummers. Late 19C. *Kent.*

LIDDEN. A story read aloud; a song; a monotonous refrain. 18C. *Somerset.*

LIGYROPHOBIA. A morbid fear of loud and sudden noises. 19C.

LILL. The hole of a wind instrument. 18C. *Scotland and N. England.*

LIP. To make a noise with the lips to attract the notice of a dog. Late 19C. *Warwicks.*

LISTENER. Slang, meaning the ear. Late 19C.

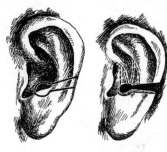

LITHOPHONE. A medical instrument for rendering audible the contact between a probe and a bladder-stone. Late 19C.

LOADIE-GRUNT. The sound made by a pig. Late 19C. *Shetland.*

LOAL. To make a strange noise; to emit a wild sort of cry as a strange cat does. Early 19C. *Scotland and N. England.*

LOLABY. A screaming child. Late 19C. *Edinburgh.*

LOLDER. To sing in a noisy, ranting manner; to make any singing noise. Late 19c. *Yorks.*

LOSH. To make the lapping sound caused by a running stream flowing over stones; to splash. Mid 19c. *Lakeland and Westmor.*

LOTTLE. To make the sound of water trickling in a small stream. Mid 19c. *Wilts.*

LOUNEN. To make a noise like that of the crane, *Grus grus. Middle English.*

LOUSTER. To make a clumsy, rattling noise; to create a commotion; to scramble noisily. 18c. *Sussex and Hants.*

LOUSTER-CROWN. One who is always causing a loud racket or commotion. Late 19c. *Hants.*

LOW-BELL. A bell formerly rung at daybreak by the herdsman appointed to take charge of cows to be turned out for grazing during the day. At the sound of the 'low-bell' the cows were delivered to him. Late 19c. *Berks.*

LOWDER. To shout or call out with a loud voice; to call out angrily. Late 19c. *E. Anglia.*

LOWER. Of a bell or clock: to strike with a prolonged sound; to toll. Mid 19c. *Devon.*

LOWN, LOWNLY. Of speech: softly, gently, in a low tone. Early 19c. *Scotland.*

LOWSEN. To listen. Mid 19c. *Dorset.*

LUDERHORN. A trumpet made of a bullock's horn, kept in a

fishing boat to be blown in foggy weather to warn all boats within hearing, or to be blown when nearing the landing to warn those ashore of the boat's approach. Late 19C. *Shetland.*

LULLER. To make an incessant noise. Late 19C. *E. Anglia.*

LUMBERMENT. A loud noise. Early 20C. *United States.*

LUN. To listen; to be still and quiet. From Norwegian dialect *luna*, to go quietly for the purposes of eavesdropping or listen-ing. Late 19C. *Shetland and Orkney.*

LUNK. To make a gurgling noise in swallowing. Late 19C. *Pembrokes.*

LURE. To utter a loud and shrill cry. Late 19C. *E. Anglia.*

LURRY. A rapid and indistinct mode of reading aloud. Late 19C. *Sussex and Hants.*

LUSHINGE. A crashing noise. *Middle English.*

LYKEWAKE-DIRGE. The song sung during a vigil over a corpse. Early 19C.

M

MADDLE. To confuse, bewilder, especially with noise; to talk incoherently. 18c. *N. England.*

MAG. To chatter, amounting somewhat to displeasure; a talkative, garrulous person; the 'mag' of 'magpie'. Mid 19c. *N. England and E. Anglia.*

MAGIC-MUSIC. A game in which a person is guided in finding a hidden article, or in doing a specific act required, by music which is made more rapid as he approaches success, and slower as he recedes. Late 19c.

MAIDEN-BELL. A bell cast to a perfect pitch. Late 19c. *Devon.*

MANDRAKE-SHRIEK. The horrible cry alleged to be emitted by the mandrake, *Bryonia alba*, on being uprooted, and which will drive all who hear it insane. 17c.

MANDREL. The rotating spindle of a phonograph, onto which a wax cylinder is placed and made to revolve during the recording or reproduction of sound. Late 19c.

MAPSE. To make a smacking noise with the lips when eating. Late 19c. *Somerset and Devon.*

MARK-HARMONICA. An instrument which assumes different shapes according to the number of performers for which it is intended, viz., if for four, the instrument may assume the form of a table; if for six, a hexagon; and if for eight, an octagon. There are separate compartments for soprano, alto, tenor and bass. The sound of each note is produced by a brass or other metallic vibrator through the agency of bellows. Mid 19c.

MARR. To purr as a cat; of an infant: to make a cooing sound. Late 19c. *Clydes.*

MARRIAGE-MUSIC. The crying and squalling of children. 17c.

MARRIAGE-SHAKE. A ticking sound, like that of a watch. Late 19c. *Shetland.*

MARROWSKYING. The use of a slang among medical students. At the London University they have a way of disguising English by transposing the initials of words, e.g. 'smoke a pipe' becomes 'poke a smipe', and 'butterfly' becomes 'flutter-bye'. This disagreeable nonsense, which has not even the recommendation of a little ability in its composition, is also termed Medical Greek. Late 19c.

MAULP. The bullfinch, *Pyrrhula pyrrhula*; so called from its low, plaintive cry. Late 19c. *Lancs.*

MAUNDER. To grumble or mutter; a beggar who uses much lamentation whilst soliciting. Early 19c.

MAY-HORN. A horn blown by boys on the first of May, made from the rind of the withy, wound round and round; a smaller piece being wound also and inserted at the smaller end. It gives forth a most doleful but far-reaching sound. Late 19c. *Berks.*

MAY-MUSIC. Music made to inaugurate the first of May, by means of whistles fashioned from the branches of the sycamore. Mid 19c. *Cornwall.*

MAY-SINGERS. Parties of young men who, a day or two before the first of May, go out in the early morning to the various farmhouses singing a song in welcome of the 'merry month'. Late 19c. *Cheshire.*

MEADOWCRAKE-CUTBOX. A machine for cutting fodder; so called for making a sound which is thought to be like the cry of the corncrake. Late 19c. *Lincs.*

MEAN. To utter a moaning sound, to wail, to bemoan; to indicate pain. Mid 19c. *Galloway and Cumber.*

MEAPEE. To show a dislike to anything by making a disagreeable sound with the lips and the mouth. 18c. *Devon.*

MELODIC-SYMPHONIUM. A musical instrument provided with a chromatic keyboard, vibrators, reeds and other sonorous bodies, and swell bellows. By this instrument any music written for violin or other instruments of that class may be played in its proper style. Its general shape resembles that of a violoncello. Mid 19c.

MELODIORGUE. An instrument with free reed stops of novel combination, and three times the power of any other keyed instrument, while its dimensions render it suitable for the smallest chapel. Mid 19c.

MEMNONIAN. Any sound that is reminiscent of the celebrated Egyptian statue near Thebes, described by the ancients as emitting a tone at sunrise similar to a lyre string breaking or the striking of brass. Early 19c.

MENAI-ECHO. A remarkable echo at the suspension bridge over the Menai Strait, whereby the blow of a hammer on one of the main piers is successively returned to each cross-beam which supports the roadway, and from the opposite pier 576 feet distant. The sound of the percussion is repeated twenty-eight times in five seconds. Mid 19C.

MEOUT. A slight sound; the least noise. Late 19C. *Scotland and Ireland.*

MERRY-WANG. A rustic form of banjo, made from a calabash sliced in two and fitted with a dried skin, to which is attached an ornamented handle and four strings. 18C. *Jamaica.*

MEWSING. The screaming of seagulls at the approach of and

during stormy weather. 'Mewsy' by extension means stormy. Late 19C. *E. Anglia.*

MEWTLE. Of cows and ewes: to make a low, crooning sound over their new-dropped young. Late 19C. *Westmor. and Cumber.*

MI-DOOVELESKO-GODLI. The sound of thunder; literally, my God's voice. Late 19C. *English Gypsy.*

MINNEER. A great noise; to make a great noise. Late 19C. *Banffs.*

MIRLITON. A kind of musical toy into which one sings, hums, or speaks, producing a coarse, reedy sound. Early 19C.

MISSION-SQUAWKER. An evangelist, one who not infrequently 'squawks' or raises his voice to unnecessary heights when exhorting his flock. Early 20C. *United States.*

MOB. The noise which small birds make at the sight of a hawk or a cat. Late 19C. *E. Anglia.*

MOLLY-O'MORGAN. Rhyming slang: a barrel organ. It may be derived from a musical-hall song beginning: 'Molly O'Morgan, with her little organ'. Late 19C. *London.*

MONKEY'S-ORPHAN. The name for the fiddler on board a naval vessel. 19C.

MONODY. A mournful ode or poem in which a single mourner bewails. 17C.

MORBLEU. To cry out; to make a great noise. Early 19C. *Dorset and Cornwall.*

MORK-SHRIEK. A 'shriek in the dark', from the former belief that ghosts walk at the witching time of night and annoy the slumbering inhabitants with loud screams; latterly a humbug or old wife's tale. Late 19C. *E. Anglia.*

MORT. A note or series of notes sounded on a horn at the death of hunted game. 16C.

MOTOPHONE. A sound-engine of Edison's actuated by aerial sound-waves. Late 19C.

MOUNTAIN-BOOMER. The red squirrel of America, *Tamiasciurus hudsonicus*; so called from the peculiar noise it makes. Mid 19C. *United States.*

MOURN. Of cattle: to utter sounds implying illness or hunger. Late 19C. *Caithness.*

MOUSE. The strongest muscle in the shoulder of a pig; which, when drawn out quickly from the flitch, makes a squeaking noise; and children often say to the butcher, 'Come, let's hear the mouse squeak.' Late 19C. *Wilts. and Northants.*

MOUSE-SNAP. A mouse trap. Early 19C. *Somerset.*

MOUTH-ALMIGHTY. A noisy, talkative person. Late 19C.

MUCK-SPOUT. One who is at once loquacious and very foul-mouthed. Late 19C. *E. Anglia.*

MUFF. To make a sound or slight noise; to speak. Late 19C. *Midlands and Yorks.*

MUMBLEMENT. Mumbling or indistinct speech. 16C.

MUM-CHANCE. A stupid, silent fellow. Late 19C. *Sussex*.

MUMP. To talk in a serious or earnest way, as in begging. Mid 19C. *London*.

MUNGING. Begging, whining; muttering. Late 19C. *N. England*.

MURRE. The common guillemot, *Uria aalge*; so called from its purring cry. Late 19C. *Cornwall and Dorset*.

MUSH. A muttered sound; a whisper. Early 19C. *Scotland and E. Anglia*.

MUSH-MOUTH. An indistinct speaker. Early 20C. *United States*.

MUSIC. The watch-word used among highwaymen, signifying the person is a friend, and must pass unmolested. Early 19C.

MUSIC-DUFFER. A dishonest seller of bad musical instruments. Mid 19C. *London*.

MUSIC-HALL-HOWL. A mode of singing in music-halls, the result of endeavouring rather to make the words of a song heard throughout the building than to create any pleasing musical effect. Late 19C.

MUSICKER. A musician, a player upon any musical instrument. Early 19C.

MUSSITATION. A symptom of the sick consisting in movement of the lips, accompanied either by the production of a faint muttering or no audible speech at all. Late 19C.

MUTE. Not giving a ringing sound when struck; said of a metal or mineral. Early 19C.

MUTES. Musicians who go about at night during Christmas time, arousing the slumbering to their devotions; the 'waits'. Mid 19C. *Lancs*.

N

NACKER. A drum. Late 19c. *Lincs.*

NAIZE. A noise; a scolding or loud disturbance. Late 19c. *Isle of Wight.*

NANG, NANGY. To gnash or grind the teeth; to make half articulate sounds by wagging the jaw in mockery. Mid 19c. *Kent, Sussex and W. England.*

NARRE. To growl like a dog. Late 19c. *Sussex.*

NATTER. A woman who works constantly at something which makes a slight noise, such as knitting. Late 19c. *Cumber.*

NATTLE. A light, quick knocking; a rattling sound; as a coal-pit term: the crackling noise made in a 'creep'. Mid 19c. *N. England.*

NATTLER. A player on the 'bones' or short pieces of sheep rib bone which, when properly held between the fingers and shaken, produce a 'nattling' noise. Early 19c. *Cumber.*

NAUTERING. Going about with music. 19c. *English Gypsy.*

NEESTERIN. A creaking noise, especially of boots. Late 19c. *Shetland.*

NEEZE. The whistling sound in breathing through the nose when one has a cold. Late 19c. *Yorks., Lancs. and Shrops.*

NEEZLE. To make the noise which accompanies a sneeze. Late 19C. *Yorks*.

NICK. To make a clicking sound. Late 19C. *Scotland and Orkney*.

NICKERERS. A slang name for new shoes, from their making a noticeable creaking noise. Mid 19C. *Roxburghs*.

NIGHTINGALE. A soldier who cries out in fear or alarm. It is a point of honour in several regiments never to cry out and become known as nightingales, whilst under the discipline of the cat of nine tails; to avoid which, they chew a bullet. Late 19C.

NIGHTINGALE-FLOOR. A kind of floor built in medieval Japan to give warning of intruders. The boards were mounted on sleeved nails so that the whole floor, when walked upon, would produce a chirruping noise likened to the song of a bird. 19C.

NINNY-NIAWING. The whinnying of a horse, especially of a sullen windless kind. Mid 19C. *Dumfries*.

NINNY-NEENO. An improvised musical instrument made by holding the leaves of certain plants against the teeth or a comb, and blowing through. Late 19C. *Cheshire*.

NITTER. To titter or giggle involuntarily with an effort to suppress or conceal the hilarity. Late 19C. *Yorks*.

NJOAG. The nasal suppressed sound made by cattle; the cry of a calf. Late 19C. *Shetland*.

NOBBINGS. Money collected through busking with a musical instrument. 19C. *English Gypsy*.

NOISE. Music, in general; a concert; also, a band or company of musicians. 16C.

NOISES. Sounds supposed to have been heard before the death of any person. Late 19C. *Dorset*.

NOISINGLI. Noise made for its own sake; of music: played with regard for loudness rather than feeling. *Middle English*.

NUCKER. To neigh. 19C. *English Gypsy.*

NUGGIE. The knocking sounds heard in the tin mines, attributed to the 'small people' or 'knockers', which indicate either the presence of mineral lodes or else give the miners warning of danger. Late 19C. *Cornwall.*

NURTH. Noise, din, racket. *Middle English.*

NUTTER. To whinny softly, as a mare and colt to one another. Late 19C. *Oxfords. and Berks.*

NYUCKFIT. The snipe, *Gallinago gallinago*; so called in imitation of its cry when ascending. Late 19C. *Clydes.*

O

Oat-pipe. A musical pipe of oat-straw; a shepherd's pipe; a pastoral song. 16c.

Obeophone. A mechanical musical instrument with a keyboard, designed to imitate or supply the sound of woodwind instruments. Early 20c.

Ollering-owl. The tawny owl, *Strix aluco*; so called from its hooting cry. Late 19c. *Sussex.*

Oob. To howl, moan, wail; a low moaning sound. Late 19c. *Shetland.*

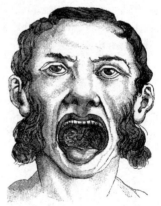

Opeidoscope. An instrument consisting of a tube having one end open and the other end covered with a thin flexible membrane to the center of which is attached a small mirror. It is used for exhibiting upon a screen, by means of rays reflected from the mirror, the vibratory motions caused by sounds produced at the open end of the tube, as by singing or speaking into it. Late 19c.

ORCHESTRINA. A large barrel organ, furnished with additional pipes to imitate various wind-instruments, and an apparatus to produce the effects of drums, triangles and cymbals. Early 19c.

ORGANUM-HYDRAULICUM. An instrument of the Romans which ought more properly to be regarded as a pneumatic organ, for the sound was produced by the current of air through the pipes, the water applied serving merely to give the necessary pressure to the bellows and to regulate their action. A representation of it is shown on a coin of the Emperor Nero.

ORGUINETTE. A mechanical musical instrument, driven by a hand-crank and equipped with reeds and bellows. The wind from the bellows passes through holes in a card, which correspond with the notes to be played. Late 19c.

ORPHORION. A metal-stringed instrument similar to a cittern, played by plucking. 16c.

OSTEOPHONE. An instrument for the transmission of auditory vibrations through the bones of the head, so as to be appreciated as sounds by persons deaf from causes other than those affecting the nervous apparatus of hearing. Late 19c.

OU. A Chinese instrument of percussion made of wood in the shape of a crouching tiger. It is hollow, and along its back are about twenty small pieces of metal, pointed, and in appearance not unlike the teeth of a saw. The performer strikes them with a sort of plectrum resembling a brush, or with a small stick called *tchen*. The tiger rests generally on a hollow wooden pedestal, about three feet six inches long, which serves as a soundboard.

OUFF. The sound of a dog barking. Late 19c. *Scotland.*

OUTCRY. Originally an auction held in a market square or outside the house of a debtor, latterly describing indoor auctions and trading where bids are shouted or otherwise made in plain view of all present. Late 19c.

OWER-TUNE. The burden of a song, corresponding to 'owerword' in a Scotch ballad. Mid 19c. *Co. Durham.*

OXYELOIA. Abnormal sensitivity to sound; excessively acute hearing. Late 19c.

P

PACK-RACKET. A species of firework constructed so as to explode with a succession of loud reports; a cracker. Late 19c. *Worcs.*

PAD-FOOT. A kind of ghost, or goblin, described as being something like a large sheep or dog. It is supposed to accompany persons on their night walks, much as a dog might, keeping by their side and making a soft noise with its feet—pad, pad, pad—whence its name. Late 19c. *Yorks.*

PALAVER. Soothing talk, generally of the high-flown kind, used by a travelling swindler; any prolonged or noisy discussion. Early 19c.

PANKER. A small pig with bad lungs that blows and wheezes like a bellows. Early 20c. *Somerset.*

PANMELODION. A keyboard musical instrument whose tone is produced by wheels rubbing on metal bars. Late 19c.

PARLY. To talk unintelligibly; to speak French. Late 19c. *Sussex.*

PAROO-DOG. A rattle made of tins, used to help muster sheep. Early 20c. *Australia.*

PARROT-COAL. A kind of domestic coal; so called from the crackling and chattering sound it makes in burning. 17c.

PASSON. The streaked gurnard, *Trigla lineata*; so called in reference to the grunt given by this fish, a corruption of the Cornish *pasor*, meaning one who coughs. Late 19C. *Cornwall.*

PATTERERS. Men who cry last dying speeches, &c., in the streets, and those who sell off their wares by long harangues in the public thoroughfares. 19C. *London.*

PATTER-FLASH. To speak the language of thieves; to talk cant. Early 19C. *London.*

PEABIRD. The wryneck, *Jynx torquilla*; so called from its sharp utterance of 'pea-pea'. Late 19C.

PEAK. To chirp as a young bird; to squeak like a mouse; to speak or sing in a thin, weak voice. Late 19C. *Midlands and Scotland.*

PEASWEEP. The greenfinch, *Carduelis chloris*; so called in imitation of its wheezing note. Late 19C.

PECH. To cough in a subdued way; to make a noise similar to the faint cough of a sheep. Late 19C. *Yorks.*

PECHEERY. A king-bird of the genus *Tyrannus*; so called from its relentless shriek, very similar to the words 'pecheery-pecheery, pe-cheer-ry'. Mid 19C. *Jamaica.*

PECTORILOQUY. The distinct articulation of the sounds of a patient's voice, heard on applying the ear to the chest in auscultation. It usually indicates some morbid change in the lungs or pleural cavity. Early 19C.

PEENT. The piping sound made by the male American woodcock, *Scolopax minor,* before and after flight. Early 20C. *United States.*

PEEP. Of a queen bee: to make a noise in the hive previous to swarming. Mid 19C. *Devon*.

PEESTER. The sound made by a mouse; a faint squeak. Late 19C. *Shetland and Orkney*.

PEETY. The smallness of a noise. Late 19C. *Kent*.

PEE-WIT. A primitive musical instrument made by boys where a small stick is split and an ivy leaf inserted, blowing on this produces a curious sound. Late 19C. *Berks*.

PEGGY-CUTTHROAT. A rustic name for the whitethroat, *Sylvia communis*; so called from its harsh note. Late 19C. *Midlands*.

PEGH. To pant; to breathe with difficulty; to sigh heavily. Mid 19C. *N. England and Scotland*.

PENNY-HOP. A country dancing club, from the custom of each person paying a penny to the fiddler. Late 19C.

PETER-DICK. A child's toy consisting of half a walnut shell, a small piece of stick and some thread. When played upon by the fingers in a particular way, it makes a ticking noise, and is supposed to say: 'Peter Dick, Peter Dick, Peter Dick's peat stack'. Late 19C. *N. Ireland*.

PEUK. To whine, wail. Late 19C. *Cumber. and Scotland*.

PHILIP. The house-sparrow, *Passer domesticus*; so called in imitation of its cry. 16C.

PHONEIDOSCOPE. An instrument for studying the motions of sounding bodies by optical means. It consists of a tube across the end of which is stretched a film of soap solution thin enough to give colored bands, the form and position of which are affected by sonorous vibrations. Late 19C.

PHONOAUTOGRAPH. An instrument for registering the changing intensity of sound, by means of a resonating diaphragm to which is attached a pig's bristle. The vibration of the diaphragm is conducted through the bristle, which in turn draws a trace on a revolving cylinder dusted with fine soot. Mid 19C.

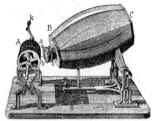

PHONOCAMPTIC. Possessing the property of reflecting sound; producing an echo. 17C.

PHONOGRAPH. An instrument by which spoken words or other sounds can be recorded, and afterwards given out again almost in the original tones. Late 19C.

PHOTOGRAPHONE. A device, consisting essentially of an electric arc and a camera, by which a series of photographs of the variations of the arc due to sound waves are obtained for reproduction by means of a selenium cell and a telephone. Early 20C.

PHTHONGOMETER. A scientific instrument for measuring vocal sounds. Mid 19C.

PHUT. To go phut: to break down or fail to work; from Hindi *phat*, meaning a crack or the sound of a slap. 19C. *Anglo-Indian.*

PIBCORN. A rustic musical instrument consisting of a wooden pipe with seven holes, surmounted by a horn at each end. It is 19 inches in length, the tone a medium between the flute and clarionet. Late 19C. *Wales and Cornwall.*

PIFFING. Sub-calibre firing on a naval gunnery range; echoic of the sound produced. Early 20C.

PIG'S WHISPER. A low or inaudible whisper. Late 19C. *Northants.*

PIKK. To tap or strike lightly so as to make a noise intended to attract the attention of others. Late 19C. *Shetland.*

PILATE-VOICE. A loud, ranting voice. Late 19C.

PILLALOO. A cry or lament at a funeral; a cry of distress. From the Gaelic *puilliliú*. Mid 19C. *Ireland*.

PINCHEM. The blue tit, *Parus coeruleus*; so called from its loud chirping cry, shrill and often repeated. Late 19C. *Bedfords*.

PING. To speak in a high, quick, singing voice. From the sharp 'ping' of the old musket. Mid 19C.

PINKETY. The chaffinch, *Fringilla coelebs*; so called from its reiterated monotonous call-note. Late 19C. *Northants*.

PINKING. The production of a rattling sound in an internal combustion engine, resulting from too rapid a combustion within the cylinder. Early 20C.

PINKLE-PANKLE. To make a tinkling sound as of a little liquid left in a bottle, jar, &c. Early 19C. *Galloway*.

PINKWINK. A tadpole; so called from the noise it is alleged to make. Late 19C. *United States*.

PIPE-DOWN. The tattoo sounded in the evening on board a naval vessel to instruct the crew to retire below decks. Mid 19C. *United States*.

PIPER. A horse that makes a wheezing noise going uphill. Late 19C. *Northum*.

PIPING. The noise made by bees preparatory to swarming. Late 19C. *Yorks. and Lancs*.

PIP-PIP. An exclamation of farewell; from the sound made by a bicycle-horn or motor-horn on departure. Early 20C.

PIPPLE. To cry, whimper. Late 19C. *Aberdeens*.

PITCAKE. A species of plover; so called in expression of the sound emitted by the bird. Late 19C. *Berwicks.*

PITCH. A fixed locality where a patterer can hold forth to a gaping multitude for at least some few minutes continuously. 19C.

PITHER. To move with a slight rustling noise. Late 19C. *Midlands.*

PITTER. To make a low shrill noise; to grieve piteously. Late 19C. *E. Anglia.*

PLANGOROUS. Resonant or plaintive in tone; characterised by loud lamentation. 16C.

PLAPPER. To make gentle repetitive sounds with the lips or by striking a flat-surfaced body in water. Late 19C. *Banffs.*

PLAY-PIPES. A boy's plaything, made from a joint of the green stalk of the bunnon or cow-parsley, or of a stout oat-stem, by cutting it two-thirds through, at intervals of about one-third or half an inch, along the greater part of its length. This instrument is played upon by blowing in at one end. Late 19C. *Yorks.*

PLEEP. To speak in a querulous, complaining tone of voice; of birds: to chirp. Late 19C. *Shetland and Orkney.*

PLING. Expressive of the sound of the harp; a vibrating sound, like a string smartly struck; to tune the strings of a fiddle. Late 19C. *Shetland and Orkney.*

PLIT-PLAT. Expressive of the sound made by a horse's hoofs as it trots along the road. Late 19C. *Cumber.*

PLOUNCE. To plunge into water with a loud noise. 17C. *Dorset and E. Anglia.*

PLOUTER. A splashing sound, as may be caused by walking through mud or water. Early 19C. *Scotland.*

PLUNDER. A noise as of articles of furniture falling or being moved. Late 19C. *Cheshire.*

PLYPE. The noise made by the fall of a body into a liquid or semi-liquid substance. Late 19C. *Aberdeens. and Banffs.*

PNEUMATOPHONY. Articulate speech supposedly uttered by a spirit or apparition. Late 19C.

POBBLE. The noise made by the bubbling of water when commencing to boil. Late 19C. *Berks.*

POLYPHONIAN-TRUMPET. A trumpet which, by means of an additional tube communicating with the main channel, is able to obtain additional tones or notes besides those called trumpet notes. Early 19C.

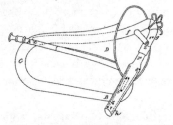

POLYPHONIST. A proficient in the art of mimicry of others'

speech; a ventriloquist. Mid 19C.

POLYPHLOESBOEAN. Loud-roaring, as of projected speech. Early 19C.

POM-POM. A one-pounder automatic machine cannon using ammunition fed from a looped belt attached to the gun; so called from its peculiar drumming sound in action. Late 19C.

POOR-WILLIE. The bar-tailed godwit, *Limosa lapponica*; so called from its whistling cry, resembling the utterance of these words. Late 19C. *Lothian.*

POP. The bell of the foxglove, *Digitalis purpurea*; so called from its making a 'popping' noise when blown out, and suddenly burst. Late 19C. *Dorset, Somerset and Hants.*

POPPYSMIC. Of the sound of the lips being smacked together in approbation. Early 20c.

PORK. To cry pork: to give intelligence to the undertaker of a funeral. A metaphor borrowed from the raven, whose note resembles the word 'pork'. Ravens are said to smell carrion at a distance. 19c.

POSHAVABEN. False laughter. Late 19c. *English Gypsy.*

POST-HORN. The nose; so called from the noise produced when it is blown. Early 19c.

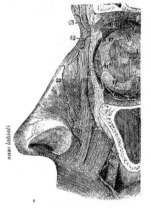

POUPEN. To make a gulping sound while drinking; to blow a horn. *Middle English.*

POUT. To make a noise when starting suddenly from under water. Early 19c. *Scotland.*

PRATE. Of a hen: to make the peculiar noise indicating she is about to lay. Late 19c. *N. England and E. Anglia.*

PRETTY-PRETTY-CREATURE. A name for the yellow-hammer, *Emberiza citrinella*; so called in imitation of its peculiarly plaintive note. Late 19c. *Gloucs.*

PSITHURISM. A whispering or faint rustling noise, as of leaves stirred by the wind. Mid 19c.

PUBLIC-PATTERERS. Swell mobsmen who pretend to be Dissenting preachers, and harangue in the open air to attract a crowd for their confederates to rob. Early 19c. *London.*

PUE. To make a low whistling sound; to chirp, as birds do. 16c.

PUG. Mortar or the like, laid between the joists under a floor, or within a partition, to deaden sound. Mid 19c.

PUIST. A groaning sound made by cattle when they are lying

down full and comfortable. Late 19c. *Northum.*

PUMP-BORER. The lesser spotted woodpecker, *Dendrocopus minor*; so called because the noise it makes is like that produced by boring with an augur through hard wood. Late 19c. *Shrops.*

PURL. To make a murmuring sound, as the water of a stream does in running over or through obstructions. 17c.

PURIFICATION. The name given in *Cumina* cult ceremonies to the rite of drumming, whereby the sound of the drums draws sky and earthbound gods through the body of a goat preparatory to sacrificing it. Early 20c. *Jamaica.*

PURRING. The noise a peg-top makes in rapid gyration. Late 19c. *Northants.*

PYROPHONE. A musical instrument invented by Eugene Kastner, in which the tones are produced by means of burning jets of hydrogen gas enclosed in graduated glass tubes. Late 19c.

Q

QUA-BIRD. Any of several wading birds, such as the rail and night-heron, found in river estuaries and mangrove swamps; so called in imitation of their call. Mid 19C. *Jamaica*.

QUACKING-CHETE. A drake or duck; literally, a quacking thing. 17C. *Thieves' slang*.

QUACKLE. The noise made in choking; the death-rattle. Early 19C. *Essex and E. Anglia*.

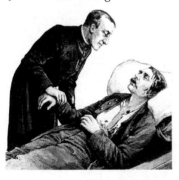

QUASE. The sound of a lyre; quavering. *Middle English*.

QUASHING. The sound made by butter when it 'comes' in churning. 18C. *Herts*.

QUEER-THE-PITCH. Inside the music-hall: to have business or applause spoiled by an interruption; so called from the patter of street performers, whose 'pitch' for performance is 'queered' by a severe policeman. Late 19C.

QUEKEN. Of geese and ducks: to honk or quack; to break wind; to make a choking sound. *Middle English*.

QUELCH. Of horses: to make a peculiar noise internally when trotting. Late 19C. *Berks*.

QUERK. To grunt; to make a noise as from pain; to let out the breath suddenly and loudly after holding it, as during strong labour. Early 19C. *Berks. and W. England.*

QUEST. The peculiar bark made by a spaniel or terrier when on a scent. The word is never used with hounds; they instead 'speak' or 'give tongue'. Late 19C. *Somerset.*

QUICKEN-WHISTLE. A whistle made by boys from a piece of the ash tree. During its fashioning, the following lines are repeated: 'Sip sap, sip sap, Willie, Willie Whitecap'. Late 19C. Lancs.

QUICK-ME-DICK. The quail, *Coturnix coturnix*; so called in imitation of its call-note. Late 19C. *Oxfords.*

QUISLE. To whistle. Late 19C. *Isle of Man.*

QUIT. Of birds and insects: to chirp. Early 20C. *United States.*

QUOBBLE. Of water: to make a noise in boiling. Late 19C. *Oxfords.*

R

RABBIT-AND-PORK. Rhyming slang for talk, usually with the meaning of incessant talk or prattling. Early 20c. *London*.

RACKAPELT. A noisy, riotous person; a barking dog. Late 19c. *Yorks., Cheshire and Lincs.*

RAIN-GOOSE. The red-throated diver, *Gavia stellata*; so named from its howling or croaking call, which is said to portend bad weather. Late 19c. *Shetland and Orkney.*

RAIRD. A clamour or noise; the act of lowing or bleating; a sudden report. 18c. *Northum. and Scotland.*

RAISING. The noise made in sustained crying or sobbing. Mid 19c. *N. England.*

RAKE. Of the sea: to break on the shore with a long, grating sound. Late 19c. *Sussex.*

RALE. A rattling sound, usually of morbid origin, accompanying the normal respiratory sounds. Early 19c.

RAMP. To eat with a gnashing sound. Late 19c. *Northum.*

RAN-TAN. A loud knocking; a noise, din. Late 19c. *Lancs. and Cheshire.*

RANDIVOOSE. A noise; an uproar, a loud commotion. Late 19c. *Devon and Cornwall.*

RAP-TAPPING. A rough amusement which consists in rousing people from sleep by a tap on their windows, and rapping their heads when they look out. Late 19c. *Yorks.*

RASH-WHISH. A whizzing sound, as of the brisk sharpening of a scythe. Late 19c. *Scotland.*

RASP. To belch. Late 19c. *E. Anglia.*

RASPER. One who speaks in a harsh, grating manner; an exasperating or annoying person. Late 19c. *Scotland and N. England.*

RASP-HOUSE. A house of correction; so called from the noise of sawing wood which emanates from within, performed by the inmates set to work. 17c.

RATAPLAN. The iterative sound of beating a drum, or of a galloping horse. Mid 19c.

RATELEN. To make a rattling sound in breathing; to speak indistinctly; of a raven: to croak. *Middle English.*

RAT-RHYME. A rhyme or piece of doggerel used in charming and killing rats; any speech repeated from memory by rote. Late 19c. *Scotland and Northum.*

RATTLE-BAG. Anything that rattles; a noisy, bustling person or one who excites alarm. The term originally denoted an instrument used for frightening horses in battle. 18c. *Scotland.*

RATTLE-BOX. An American herb, *Crotalaria sagittalis*, the seeds of which, when ripe, rattle in the inflated pod. Early 19c. *United States.*

RATTLE-CAN. A noisy person. Late 19c. *Lancs. and Cumber.*

RATTLE-SHOT. A gun-shot which is fired as a salute. Early 19c. *Renfrews.*

RATTLE-TRAP. A clattering noise. Late 19c. *Devon.*

RATTLE-WINGS. The goldeneye duck, *Bucephela clangula*; so called from the whistling made by its wings in flight. Late 19c. *Norfolk.*

RATTLER. Any vehicle notorious for making a rattling noise when in motion, humorously suggestive of rickety construction or poor maintenance; originally applied to coaches and, more recently, to railway trains. 18c.

RATTOCK. To make a great noise; a metathesis of 'racket', and probably meant to give more force to it. Late 19c. *E. Anglia.*

RAVE. Of the wind: to make a wild, rushing sound. 18c. *Ayrshire.*

RAWL. To sing tunelessly, to bawl. Late 19c. *Isle of Man.*

RAZOO. Noise showing disapproval, especially in a theatre. Late 19c. *United States.*

REACH. Of pigs: to squeal or make a noise of complaint. Late 19c. *Worcs.*

REAM. To shout, cry aloud, bawl; to talk wildly. 18c. *Scotland and N. England.*

REASTY-CROPPED. Rough of speech; hoarse-voiced. Late 19c. *Yorks.*

REBOANT. Resounding loudly. Early 19c.

REEK. To shout, scream, shriek; a shriek; a noise. Mid 19c. *Yorks. and Lancs.*

REEL. The grasshopper warbler, *Locustella naevia*; so called from the resemblance of its song to the noise of the reel employed by hand spinners of wool. Late 19C. *Norfolk*.

REEMISH. A loud, rumbling noise; especially the sound caused by a body falling. 18C. *N. Scotland*.

REEMLE-RAMMLE. To make a great deal of noise; to behave in a noisy, frolicking manner. Late 19C. *Banffs*.

REEN. To squeak or squeal as a pig. Late 19C. *Shetland*.

REESHLE. To rustle; to make a clattering, cracking sound. Early 19C. *Northum. and Scotland*.

REEZHAGH. Smooth of sound. Late 19C. *Isle of Man*.

RERE. Noise, clamour. *Middle English*.

RESONATOR. An invention of the eminent scientist Helmholtz, unequalled in simplicity and precision, for the analysis of sound, specifically timbre. The resonator is a hollow sphere of glass or of brass, its dimensions being so calculated as to furnish a given sound. It has two orifices, the larger intended to communicate with the surrounding air, the smaller, funnel-shaped, to be introduced into the ear. Mid 19C.

RHONCHISONANT. Making a snorting or snoring noise. 17C.

RHONCHUS. An adventitious whistling or snoring sound heard on auscultation of the chest when the air channels are partially obstructed. Early 19C.

RICK. To rattle, jingle; to chatter; the noise made by a polecat or ferret. 18C. *Cheshire, Yorks. and Lancs.*

RICKING-RIPE. Dead ripe; applied to corn, probably because it then makes a rattling noise. Late 19C. *Cheshire.*

RIFT. To belch, eructate. Mid 19C. *Yorks. and Co. Durham.*

RILL. To break wind. 19C. *English Gypsy.*

RIMPLE. The sound produced by a ripple of water. Late 19C. *Yorks.*

RING-AWK. Bells are 'rung awk' to give alarm of fire, meaning rung in a hurried or confused way. Late 19C. *E. Anglia.*

RINGING-GLASS. The belief a sailor will drown if a drinking-glass is tapped accidentally and so made to ring. The effect will be averted if a finger is immediately placed on the rim of the glass to halt its ringing. Late 19C.

RINGING-IN. A practice among the meat-porters of Smithfield Market, whereby if any of their number arrives for work late and attempts to do so unnoticed, he is thwarted by the massed banging of knives and other metal implements. Early 20C. *London.*

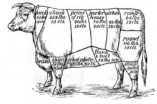

RIP. A shout; to shout. Late 19C. *Isle of Man.*

RIPON-HORN. The horn which is blown each evening at 9 p.m. in Ripon. Four blasts on the horn are given in succession from different directions around the obelisk in the market square. 19C. *Yorks.*

RIPPIT. A great noise; a noisy party. Early 20C. *United States.*

RISK. A harsh, grating sound, like the tearing of roots. Early 19C. *Scotland.*

RITTLE. To wheeze, snore; to make a rattling noise inside the throat. 18C. *Devon.*

ROARING. The continuous lowing of a herd of cattle. Early 20C. *Australia.*

ROCKER. To talk. 19C. *English Gypsy.*

ROCKEROPEN. Conversation, speech. 19C. *English Gypsy.*

ROGGELING. A loud rumbling noise. *Middle English.*

ROGUE'S-MARCH. Music played when drumming a soldier from a regiment, or driving any one away in disgrace. Early 20C.

ROGUE'S-SALUTE. The firing of a single gun that precedes a naval court-martial. Early 20C.

ROLLY. To resound, re-echo. Late 19C. *Worcs.*

ROOKAW. An instrument comprised of two jagged sticks rubbed together to make a rhythmic rattling. 18C. *Jamaica.*

ROOKERY. A noisy disturbance; a fuss; chattering. Early 19C. *Sussex, Kent and Scotland.*

ROTE. The noise produced by the surf of the sea dashing upon the shore. 17C.

ROOTLE. To rattle. Late 19C. *Essex.*

ROUGH-MUSIC. A clatter of sticks, pots, pans, and musical instruments for the annoyance of offenders outraging public prejudice; sometimes accompanied by burning in effigy. Late 19C.

ROUNGE. A great noise. Early 19C. *Northum. and Cumber.*

ROUP. To drink or gulp down liquid in a noisy manner. Late 19C. *Cornwall.*

ROUPIT. To be suffering from any affliction of the throat or chest which renders the voice hoarse. Early 19C. *Scotland.*

ROUPY-WEATHER. Misty, foggy weather that makes one hoarse-voiced. Late 19C. *Yorks.*

ROUSER. Anything resounding; a loud explosion, as of cannon fire. Late 19C. *S. England.*

ROUT. To low loudly as cattle; to bray as a donkey; to bellow, roar; to make any loud noise. Mid 19C. *Scotland and N. England.*

ROUTINGE. The loud noise of a missile in flight; whirring, whizzing. *Middle English.*

ROW-DOW. The sparrow, *Passer montanus*; so called from a peculiar habit of the bird, imitating the sound of a drum. Late 19C. N*orthants.*

ROXLE. To grunt; to speak with a hoarse voice. Late 19C. *Scotland.*

RUCKETTING. A noise made as by rats or other animals scratching boards. Late 19C. *Berks.*

RUCKSEL. A noise, clatter. Late 19C. *Devon and Cornwall.*

RUDDY. To make a loud, reiterated noise; as of the wind, expressive of the loud irregular noise it makes, especially when striking upon any object that conveys the sound, as on a door or a window. Late 19C. *N. Scotland.*

RUFF. To applaud by making noise with the hands or feet. Mid 19C. *W. Scotland.*

RUFFLE. A rapidly vibrating drumbeat; the crackling noise produced by flourishing a deck of cards. 18C.

RUMBA-BOX. A musical instrument which consists of four pieces of metal of various widths, attached to a resonating box. They vibrate when plucked with the fingers and produce tones corresponding to those of the bass viol. Early 20C. *Jamaica.*

RUMBLE-SEAT. An uncovered seat for servants positioned behind a carriage. Early 19C.

RUMBLE-TUMBLE. The rumbling sound made by rushing water, as a stream in full spate. Late 19C. *Lothian.*

RUMBLER. An octagonal box in which castings are put to be cleaned, this being effected by the revolution of the box. Late 19c. *Yorks*.

RUMBLING-KIRN. A gully on a wild rocky shore into which the tide flows with a loud noise. Early 19c. *Scotland*.

RUMPUM-SCRUMPUM. A rude kind of musical instrument made of a piece of board, with an old tin tied across it as a bridge, over which the strings are strained. It is played like a banjo, or sometimes with a sort of fiddle-bow. Late 19c. *Wilts*.

RUMPUS. The rumbling noise heard in a rabbit's or fox's burrow, when a terrier drives them out. Late 19c. *Pembrokes*.

RUNCH. The noise made by a sharp instrument piercing the flesh. Early 19c. *Galloway*.

RUNNING-STATIONER. A seller of books, ballads, dying speeches, and newspapers. Persons of this class formerly used to run with their newspapers, blowing a horn. Nowadays the last of these peripatetic newsmen bawls the heads of telegrams. Mid 19c.

RUNT. To hum, whistle. Late 19c. *Cheshire*.

RUTE. To cry with vehemence; to strive, as children do sometimes in crying, to make as much noise as they can. Mid 19c. *Cheshire*.

RUTTLE. A rattling sound in the throat arising from difficulty of breathing. 18c.

S

SANNY. To utter a whining and wailing cry without apparent cause. Late 19C. *E. Anglia.*

SAP-WHISTLE. A whistle made of a twig of the plane tree, when the bark will peel off. Mid 19C. *Co. Durham.*

SAUM. A singing noise, such as may be imagined inside the head. Late 19C. *Lincs.*

SAW-GOURDS. To snore; imitative of the sound. Late 19C. *United States.*

SAW-SHARPENER. The great tit, *Parus major*; so called from its peculiar, harsh, grating call notes. Late 19C. *Roxburghs.*

SCALE. The sound of waves breaking upon the shore. Late 19C. *Orkney.*

SCALLIBRAT. A tiresome and screaming child; to use loud and vituperative language. Late 19C. *Yorks.*

SCANKY. Shrill of sound. Late 19C. *Isle of Man.*

SCAPE. Used to express the cry of a snipe when disturbed or alarmed. Late 19C. *Norfolk, Surrey and Somerset.*

SCART. The cormorant, *Phalocrocorax carbo*; so called from its rasping call. 16C.

SCAT. The sound of a rent; a sharp sound as of a bullet. Late 19C. *Cornwall.*

SCATTER-BASKET. A clattering noise, as made by a wheel when it requires tightening. Late 19C. *Devon.*

SCAVEL-AN-GOW. The noise of confused talking; chatter; scolding. Late 19C. *Cornwall.*

SCHLEMOZZLE. A loud quarrel; a noise or fuss of any kind. Late 19C. *London Jewish.*

SCISSOR-GRINDER. The nightjar, *Caprimulgus europaeus*; so called from the strange whirring, jarring noise uttered by the bird on summer evenings. Late 19C. *Norfolk and Suffolk.*

SCOLDER. The oyster-catcher, *Haematopus ostralegus*; so called perhaps from the loud and shrill noise made when any one approaches its young. 18C. *Orkney.*

SCOLDING-WIFE. A rattle, as used by a watchman or for the purpose of frightening rabbits. Late 19C. *Lincs.*

SCOUR. A noise, tumult. Late 19C. *Somerset.*

SCRAME. To make a rasping noise, as a cart or harness which needs oiling. Late 19C. *Essex.*

SCRANCH. To grind with the teeth, and with a crackling sound. 18C.

SCRANNEL-PIPING. Producing a weak, screeching noise; a feeble and discordant music; a weak, piping voice. Mid 19C. *Notts.*

SCRATE. To make a scratching noise as with a slate pencil. Late 19C. *Yorks.*

SCREAMER. A very long stroke in golf, from the whirring noise made by the ball; a whistling artillery shell or bomb. Late 19C.

SCREECH-BIRD. The fieldfare, *Turdus pilaris*. Late 19C. *Scotland.*

SCREECH-COCK. The misselthrush, *Turdus viscivorus*. Late 19C. *N. Ireland.*

SCREECH-DEVIL. The swift, *Cypselus apus*. Late 19C. *Wilts.*

SCREECH-DROSLE. The misselthrush, *Turdus viscivorus*. Late 19C. *Gloucs.*

SCREECH-HAWK. The nightjar, *Caprimulgus europaeus*. Late 19C. *Berks.*

SCREEK. To utter suddenly a sharp, shrill sound; to screech; to creak, as a door or wheel. 16C.

SCRIVE. To make a harsh sound by scratching metal. Late 19C. *Yorks.*

SCROINOCH. A shrill cry; a yell; a noisy person. 18C. *Banffs. and Aberdeens.*

SCROOP. To creak, squeak; to make a noise from friction. Mid 19C. *W. England.*

SCROOCH. A dull, scraping sound; the noise made by un-greased machinery or by moving a pointed instrument over a hard, smooth surface. Late 19C. *Kent.*

SCRUMP. To emit a crisp, crackling sound; to bite with a noise. Late 19C. *Warwicks. and Berks.*

SCRUNT. To produce a harsh noise by rubbing or scraping; to grate. Early 19C. *Clydes. and Yorks.*

SCRUPETTY. To creak, grate, make a grinding noise. Late 19C. *Wilts.*

SEA-CALF. The common seal, *Phoca vitulina*; so called from the supposed resemblance of its voice to that of a calf. 16C.

SEA-CANARY. The beluga or white whale, *Delphinapterus leucas*; so called from a whistling sound which it makes. Late 19C.

SEA-ECHO. An echo which proceeds from the sea-waves or from the sails of a ship. The report of a gun on board ship is often repeated by the surging billows leeward of the vessel, and commands uttered loudly through a speaking-trumpet are occasionally repeated by the convex surface of a sail. Mid 19C.

SEA-MEW. The common gull,

Larus canus; so called from its cry. Late 19c. *Scotland*.

SEA-ROARER. Any large whelk-shell; so called from the sound heard when placed on the ear. Late 19c. *Northum*.

SELBORNE-ECHO. A polysyllabic echo near Selborne, in the King's field leading to Norehill, which used to repeat up to ten syllables distinctly if quick dactyls were chosen, e.g. 'Know ye the land of the cypress and myrtle?' The reverberation took place from a stone building at a distance of 258 yards. Mid 19c.

SEMEIO-MELODION. An instrument which demonstrates the principles of musical writing in a visible and audible manner. It consists of a dial plate exhibiting the five horizontal lines of the stave, and furnished with a series of moveable dots or buttons, each of them representing one of the notes of the stave. The instrument is furnished with a pair of bellows

and valves with vibrating blades for giving the required sounds of the notes shown on the dial plate. Mid 19c.

SEMISOUN. A slight or soft sound. *Middle English*.

SENSITIVE-FLAMES. Flames that are easily affected by sounds. Mid 19c.

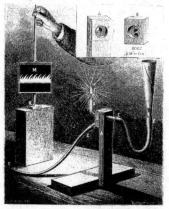

SERAPHINE. A wind instrument whose sounding parts are reeds, consisting of a thin tongue of brass playing freely through a slot in a plate. It has a case, like a piano, and is played by means of a similar keyboard, the bellows being worked by the foot. Mid 19c.

SEVEN-WHISTLERS. A flock of lapwings or whimbrels, the calls of which are said to warn of impending death or other calamity. 19C.

SHACKLERS. The seed-pods of the ash tree, *Fraxinus excelsior*, and also the field maple, *Acer campestre*; so called from the 'shackling' or rattling sound they produce. Late 19C. *Devon*.

SHALLAL. A serenade of kettles and pans given to a notorious wedding couple; a great noise. Late 19C. *Cornwall*.

SHALMEN. Of a duck: to make a noise like that of a woodwind instrument. *Middle English*.

SHANDY-FOO. To holler, shout; to make a great noise. Late 19C. *Wilts*.

SHAWM. To scream shrilly and vociferously. It appears to be formed from some resemblance, real or imagined, to the sound of the wind instrument so named, and which is supposed to have been a sort of hautboy or cornet. 19C. *E. Anglia*.

SHELENGRO. One who whistles. Late 19C. *English Gypsy*.

SHELL-BLOW. The times for starting and stopping work on a plantation, marked by the loud blowing of a conch shell. Mid 19C. *Jamaica*.

SHELTA. A kind of cryptic Irish spoken by tinkers and confirmed tramps; a secret jargon composed chiefly of Gaelic words disguised by changes of initial, transposition of letters, back-slanging, and similar devices. Late 19C.

SHEPHERD'S-HARP. Any small musical instrument that is often played in solitude, such as a tin whistle or trump. Early 20C. *Australia*.

SHEPHERD'S-WHISTLE. A kind of whistle made from a small piece of tin folded flat with a nail hole through the centre. Early 20C. *Australia*.

SHIFTING-DULLNESS. A dull sound, when elicited from the

thorax by percussion, changes its position at successive medical examinations. Mid 19c.

SHILL. Of the wind: to howl, to whistle with a shrill sound. Early 19c. *Yorks.*

SHINDY. A noisy disturbance. 19c. *English Gypsy.*

SHIPLEY-ECHO. A simple polysyllabic echo on the north side of Shipley church in Sussex, which renders as many as twenty-one consecutive syllables. Mid 19c.

SHIRL. A metathesized form of 'shrill'. Late 19c. *N. England.*

SHIVAREE. A burlesque, boisterous serenade for newlyweds with horns, bells, drums, &c. Early 19c. *United States.*

SHOE-LEATHER. The warning cry of a thief when he hears footsteps. Mid 19c. *London.*

SHOLL. To whistle. Late 19c. *English Gypsy.*

SHORK. To make a gurgling noise; the noise a person's shoes make when walking with them full of water. Late 19c. *Northum.*

SHREDCOCK. The fieldfare, *Turdus pilaris*; so called from its harsh cry uttered before the onset of rain. Late 19c. *Shrops.*

SHRICK. To shriek, as applied to the badger's cry made at rutting time. Mid 19c.

SHRIEKER. The black-tailed godwit, *Limosa limosa*; so called from its piercing cry. Early 20c. *E. Anglia.*

SHUCK-SHACK. The noise caused by walking in wet stockings. Late 19c. *Pembrokes.*

SHUD. A low, continuous sound; generally used of a noise in the distance. Late 19c. *Shetland.*

SHUTTLEBAG. When a man is husky from phlegm in his throat, he is said to have 'swallowed a shuttlebag'. Mid 19c.

SIBILACIOUN. A hissing or whistling sound. *Middle English.*

SIFE. To make a sighing noise as of the wind. Mid 19c. *Devon.*

SIFFLEMENT. The act of whistling or hissing; a whistling sound; sibilation. 17C.

SIGNAL-TRUMPET. A contrivance in which a pistol or other firearm may, by means of a screw-thread, be attached to a speaking-trumpet of brass or any other suitable material. The discharge of the firearm produces an explosion, the sound of which is accordingly increased and directed usefully, as on board ships leading ahead in fogs and in all situations of distress. 18C.

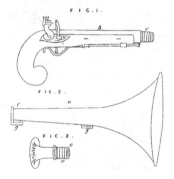

SIMPHONIE. A stringed musical instrument, especially a hurdy-gurdy; a pleasing combination of sounds; harmony, melody. *Middle English.*

SING-OF-THE-SHORE. The sound made by waves breaking on a stretch of shore and indicating its particular arrangements of sand, pebbles, boulders, cliffs, reefs and ledges of rock. Thus the experienced fisherman may glean an indication of his position when fog or darkness make land or lights invisible. Late 19C. *Cornwall.*

SING-ROVINGS. Of a cat: to purr. Late 19C. *Leics.*

SINGERATION. A musical party. Late 19C. *Wilts.*

SINGING-BIRD. The thrush, *Turdus musicus.* Late 19C. *Herefs.*

SINGING-FLAME. A flame, as of hydrogen or coal gas, burning within a tube and so adjusted as to set the air within the tube in vibration, causing sound. The apparatus is called also chemical harmonicon. Mid 19C.

SINGING-HINNY. A currant-cake baked on a girdle; so called from the singing noise emitted while it bakes over the fire. Late 19C. *N. England.*

SINGING-SPANISH. Making a wild, crooning noise; probably suggested by the church services of Queen Mary Tudor's husband. 19C.

SIRDON. A low, murmuring, plaintive cry; to emit a plaintive cry, as some birds do. Late 19C. *Scotland.*

SISS. To make a hissing sound; to make a hissing noise with which to incite a dog to the attack. 18C. *N. England.*

SISSERARA. A violent rebuking or scolding. Mid 19C. *Co. Durham.*

SISSING-MEDICINE. An effervescent draught; so called from its sound. Late 19C. *Lincs.*

SIZZING. Yeast or barm; so called from the sound made by beer or ale in working. 18C. *Sussex, Kent and Surrey.*

SIZZLER. A cook, a stove; one who works, or that which is used,

where sizzling sounds are heard. Early 20C. *United States.*

SKELDERING. Screaming, yelling. Late 19C. *Yorks.*

SKERRY-KABBERISH. A great noise; a racket; a noisy frolic. Late 19C. *Cornwall.*

SKEYLD. The sound of gentle wavelets or ripples breaking on the beach. Late 19C. *Shetland.*

SKIMMINGTON. A serenade of rough music from tin pots and pans got up to express disapproval in cases of great scandal or immorality. Early 19C. *W. England.*

SKIRLCOCK. The missel-thrush, *Turdus viscivorus*; so called from its harsh alarm note. Late 19C. *Derbys.*

SKIRL-IN-THE-PAN. The frizzling sound made by butter when it is frying in a pan. Early 19C. *Scotland.*

SKIRLAG. A child's toy consisting of a long thin leaf of corn or lyme grass, which is held between the thumbs, and on being blown makes a kind of musical note. Late 19C. *Caithness.*

SKIRLIE-WEEACK. To cry with a shrill voice; a little person with a shrill voice. Late 19C. *Banffs.*

SKREEL. To cry, shriek, squeal. Late 19C. *Sussex, Northum. and Lincs.*

SKRIKE. A scream, a sharp cry, a shriek. Mid 19C. *Co. Durham and Yorks.*

SKROKE. To make a harsh, grating noise. Late 19C. *Lakeland.*

SKROL. To scream, shriek; to bellow; of the wind: to roar loudly. Late 19C. *Shetland and Orkney.*

SKRURK. A shriek. Late 19C. *Yorks.*

SLAGGER. The act of making a gurgling noise in the throat; the growl of a dog. Late 19C. *Clydes.*

SLARG. To make a noise by rubbing with the feet. Late 19C. *Lincs.*

SLAMMOCK. With a loud noise or heavy bump. Late 19C. *Lincs.*

SLANGING. Music-hall singing; so called due to the quantity of spoken slang between the verses. Late 19C.

SLATTER. A clatter; the sound of hoofs upon hard ground. Late 19C. *Westmor.*

SLATTER-CUM-DRASH. A great noise, an uproar. Late 19C. *Devon and Cornwall.*

SLEDGE. To make a noise by rubbing the boot soles on a hard floor. Late 19C. *Yorks.*

SLEEP. Of a churn: to produce no sound when the cream is agitated. Late 19C. *Midlands and N. England.*

SLEPI-NOISE. The sound of snoring. *Middle English.*

SLIGERIN. A great noise of fighting and tumbling. Late 19C. *Cornwall.*

SLIPPETIN. Going along quickly and without noise in treading. Late 19C. *Berks.*

SLOBBER. To weep noisily. Late 19C. *Cumber.*

SLOP. The sound made by a blow. Late 19C. *Notts.*

SLORP. To make a noise with the lips whilst eating or drinking; to do anything in a noisy, slatternly way; of shoes: to make a noise which resembles sucking; a gulp. Early 19C. *Scotland and N. England.*

SLOSH. A muddy wash of water which makes a loud noise when splashed about, as distinct from 'slush' or liquid mud, which makes a duller sound. Late 19C. *Sussex.*

SLUGHORN. A rallying war-cry, such as the old Border shout of

'Yet-yet-yet'. Early 19C. *Northum.*

SLUM. Loose talk or cant. From slumber, hence slumberous talk and, by extension, a slum is also a place in which are found persons who talk in that drawling, drowsy style. Early 19C. *London.*

SLUMP. A dull obtuse noise produced by anything falling into a hole, or into a soft, miry place. 18C. *Scotland.*

SLUT. A noise; a loud sound. Late 19C. *Hants.*

SMACK. Of an eel: to utter a peculiar sound when feeding by night on the water's surface. Late 19C. *Norfolk.*

SMUCKSIN. A clattering noise. Late 19c. *Shetland.*

SNACK. The crack of a whip or any similar loud noise. Mid 19c. *Devon and Somerset.*

SNAGGER. To snore with a harsh, grating sound. Late 19c. *Scotland.*

SNAPPER. To crackle; to make a sharp, short sound. Mid 19c. *Berks.*

SNAPPING-TONGS. A game similar to 'musical chairs', where the players stand in a room in which there are chairs for all but one. When the tongs are snapped they run to sit down, and the one who fails to secure a seat pays a forfeit. Late 19c. *Dorset.*

SNAVEL. To talk or sing with a nasal tone. Mid 19c. *Yorks.*

SNICKER. The low noise made by a mare to call her foal to her side. Late 19c. *E. Anglia.*

SNICKUP. To hiccup; to sneeze; to retch noisily. Early 20c. *United States.*

SNIFFER. The porpoise, *Phocaena phocaena*; so called from the sound of its blowing. Late 19c. *Cornwall.*

SNIFTING-VALVE. A small valve opening into the atmosphere from the cylinder or condenser of a steam engine, to allow the escape of air when the piston makes a stroke; so called from the noise made by its action. Early 19c.

SNIPPETY. Journals made up of snippings from other and generally ancient journals. Used in satire; from the noise made by scissors in the operation of editing. Late 19c.

SNIRT. To laugh in a suppressed manner; to make a noise through the nose when endeavouring to restrain laughter. 18c. *Scotland and N. England.*

SNOACH. To make a snuffling noise; to speak or breathe through the nose; to snore. Late 19c. *Dorset and Somerset*.

SNOCK. The short sound of a sudden blow. Early 19c. *Dorset*.

SNOOK. The peculiar sneezing sound made by dogs burrowing in search of rats, &c. 18c. *Northum*.

SNORICK. A child's toy made from the larger bone of a pig's foot and two worsted strings. By twisting this round and then alternately straining and slackening the strings the bone is made to revolve rapidly, giving a snoring sound. Late 19c. *Caithness, Shetland and Orkney*.

SNORTER. The wheatear, *Saxicola oenanthe*; so called from its short, harsh note. Late 19c. *Dorset*.

SNURR. Of a plough: to make a low, purring sound as it is drawn through the soil. Late 19c. *United States*.

SNUSH. To sniff with a snorting sound. Late 19c. *Shetland*.

SNYIRK. To creak; to make a grating noise. Late 19c. *Shetland*.

SOAM. To make a humming or buzzing noise. Late 19c. *Notts*.

SOB. Of the wind: to make the sighing sound which announces that calmer weather is superseding a storm. 18c. *Ayrshire, Northum. and Yorks*.

SODDERING. The noise of bubbling made by boiling porridge, &c. Late 19c. *Lakeland*.

SOITL. To make a noise in drinking, applied chiefly to a pig drinking. Late 19c. *Shetland*.

SOLCH. The noise made by falling on a morass or damp place; to fall heavily and loudly. 18c. *Lancs. and Cheshire*.

SONANCE. The sounding of an instrument. 17c.

SONIFER. A kind of ear trumpet for the deaf, or the partially deaf. Late 19c.

SONOMETER. An instrument for measuring sounds and their

intervals by means of a sounding-board with moveable bridges and strings stretched above it, and weights for varying the tension. Early 19c.

SONORESCENCE. The emission of sound resulting from the intermittent action of light radiation. It is utilised in the photophone for communication. Late 19c.

SONOROUS-TUMOR. A tumor which emits a clear, resonant sound on percussion. Late 19c.

SOO. A whistling sound; the sound of the wind or water; a whirring, as of machinery. Mid 19c. *Cheshire, Yorks. and Lancs.*

SOOM. To drink hastily, and make a noise with the lips in so doing. Late 19c. *Leics., Westmor. and Lakeland.*

SOTTLE. Expressive of the sound made by any soft substance, as porridge, broth, &c., when boiling. Late 19c. *Ayrshire.*

SOUFFLE. A murmuring or blowing sound heard on auscultation; as of the uterine souffle heard over the pregnant uterus. Late 19c.

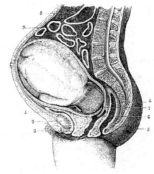

SOUGH. To whistle or sigh, as the wind. *Middle English.*

SOUL-BELL. That bell which was formerly rung while the sick lay in extremity, to admonish those who heard it to pray for the soul while it was passing. Late 19c. *E. Anglia.*

SOULING. A custom on the 1st and 2nd November, All Saints' Day and All Souls' Day respectively. Parties of young people visit houses and sing in the hope of collecting money or other gifts. The song begins: 'Soul, soul for a souling cake. I pray you, missis, for a souling cake'. Early 19c. *Cheshire, Lancs. and Shrops.*

SOUND-REFLECTOR. An apparatus of a nature similar to that used in reflecting light. It is applied to an ordinary steam whistle for the purpose of concentrating and throwing out the sound vibrations produced by the whistle all around in a horizontal plane, or for projecting them in one direction. Mid 19C.

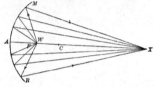

SOUNINGE. Making sound; a pleasant sound; speech. *Middle English.*

SPARRE. To cry out at the market-place. *Middle English.*

SPEAK. Of a hound: to bark when the game is found. Late 19C. *Somerset.*

SPEAKEASY. A resort in which illicit liquor is served, the name being given because patrons desiring to gain entrance are usually forced to whisper or 'speakeasy' their name, or that of their sponsor, before gaining admittance. Also, a shotgun as used by law officers and prison guards, being a jocular reference to the roar of such a weapon when discharged. Early 20C. *United States.*

SPEAWKER. A toy consisting of a tube made of the hollow bark of a wicken-twig, removed intact from the wood by means of light hammering. It produces a shrill, shrieking noise when blown through. Late 19C. *Lancs.*

SPHYGMOPHONE. A medical instrument by means of which a pulse-beat makes a sound. Mid 19C.

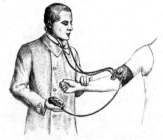

SPIELER. A public speaker or lecturer. Late 19C. *United States.*

SPITHEAD-NIGHTINGALE. The bo'sun's pipe. The trilling of these pipes can be heard for miles when the Fleet is lying at Spithead. Early 20C.

SPLORROCH. The sound made by walking in the wet or mud. Late 19C. *Ayrshire.*

SPLOTHER. A splashing noise. Late 19C. *Worcs.*

SPRAECH. To cry with a loud, shrill sound; to wail, lament. Late 19c. *Shetland.*

SPRALLICH. To cry loudly, to shriek; a loud, shrill cry. Late 19c. *Banffs.*

SPRIG. A tune, piece of music. Late 19c. *Aberdeens. and Perths.*

SPUR-PEAL. The peal of church bells made on the evening of the Sunday when the banns of marriage are published for the first time. Mid 19c. *Lincs.*

SPURRE. The common tern, *Sterna flaviatilis*; so called from the sound of its cry. Late 19c. *Cornwall and Pembrokes.*

SQUACKET. To quack as a duck; to make any disagreeable sound with the mouth. Late 19c. *Surrey, Sussex and Somerset.*

SQUAICH. A loud scream, especially the cry of wildfowl or of an animal being caught. Early 19c. *N. Ireland, W. Scotland and Caithness.*

SQUALLOCH. To scream; a person with noisy manners and a shrill voice. Early 19c. *Aberdeens. and Banffs.*

SQUASHLE. To make a splashing noise, as feet do in wet shoes. Late 19c. *Kent.*

SQUAT. To quieten down; to put to silence, as with a fretful child. Hence squatting-pill, an opiate in the form of a pill. Late 19c. *E. Anglia.*

SQUATCH. To make a slight noise. Late 19c. *Oxfords. and Berks.*

SQUAWKING-THRUSH. A name for the missel-thrush, *Turdus viscivorus.* Mid 19c. *Isle of Wight.*

SQUEAKER. Any of various birds or insects, especially the cicada, which make a squeaking noise. Early 20c. *Australia.*

SQUEAN. Of swine: to make a restless, fretful noise. 18c. *Midlands and Northants.*

SQUEAPITY. To squeak, as an ungreased wheel. Mid 19c. *Dorset.*

SQUEEGEE. A mud-clearer, consisting of a plate of vulcanised india-rubber fixed at right angles to a long handle; echoic of the noise produced during its use. Mid 19c.

SQUILKER. To make a noise indicative of having liquid inside. Late 19c. *Notts. and Leics.*

SQUIRREL-HUNTING. A curious custom, in which the young men of Duffield gather on the first Monday of November, and with pots, frying-pans, &c., proceed in search of squirrel. They gather themselves round oaks and elms and, with the noise of their instruments, soon succeed in starting one amongst the boughs. This they chase from tree to tree, until stunned by the noise and wearied with exertion, it falls to the ground and is thus captured. The squirrel is then carried in triumph back to Duffield. Mid 19c. *Derbys.*

SQUIT. To make a very brief, slight sound. Late 19c. *Dorset.*

STAND-FROM-UNDER. A slang term, chiefly used in the theatrical world, for thunder. Derived from the naval command to 'stand from under', used when a heavy object is to be lowered or dropped from above. Many former sailors found work in the theatrical profession as scene-shifters. Early 20c.

STAUPINGS. The sound of footsteps. Late 19c. *Yorks.*

STEINKLE. The wheatear, *Saxicola oenanthe*; so called from the similarity of its note to the 'chinking' sound of two pebbles struck together. Late 19c. *Shetland and Orkney.*

STENTOROPHONIC. Speaking or sounding very loud; stentorian. 19c.

STEVEN, STEVIN. A voice, especially a loud voice; a ranting. 18c. *Scotland and N. England.*

STEVENING. Noise, sound. *Middle English.*

STEWED-PRUNE. From rhyming slang: a tune, typically used in requesting a musician to play, as in 'Give us a stewed prune'. Late 19C. *London.*

STHOO. To chase with opprobrious shouting. Late 19C. *Isle of Man.*

STICHLE. To rustle, as papers disturbed by the quest of a mouse; to emit a sound like that of snoring. Early 19C. *Aberdeens. and Renfrews.*

STIGMATA. The external organs of respiration of flies, consisting of minute apertures. The buzzing of the fly depends on the rapid escape of air through the stigmata during the muscular effort of flying. 18C.

STOCK-AND-HORN. A rough musical instrument composed of a sheep's thigh-bone, with six or seven ventiges, attached to a cow's horn. It is played with an oaten reed, not made fast in the bone, but held by the lips. 18C. *Ayrshire and Lanarks.*

STOUND. To beat a drum; to sound, resound; to clang. Early 19C. *Scotland and N. England.*

STRAM. To slam, bang; to put down or close violently and noisily. 18C. *W. England.*

STRAMASH. An uproar; a noisy crash; a loud explosion. Early 19C. *Scotland and N. England.*

STREET-YELP. A passing street cry, such as 'Does your mother know you're out?' Every week some new street yelp is invented, and eagerly taken up as a substitute for wit by the class that enjoys these things. Late 19C.

STREPENT. Noisy, dissonant. 18C.

STRIKE-A-LIGHT. In American sailing ships, the order from the mate to start the shanty man singing. 19c.

STRIKER. A spectral hound said to be encountered wherever calamity is at hand, or where some accident or evil deed may have occurred; so called in allusion to the sound of its voice, like hammer-blows, when heard by those persons who are unable to see the appearance itself. Late 19c. *Lancs.*

STRIM-STRUM. Unmusical; a worn-out instrument. Late 19c. *Wilts. and Somerset.*

STRUNCHEON. The verse of a song. Mid 19c. *Lincs.*

SUILK. To make a sucking noise with the mouth. Late 19c. *Shetland.*

SUMPHION. A musical instrument; a kind of drum. Mid 19c. *Scotland.*

SUTHER. To sigh, especially used of the wind among trees; of an organ: to make a blowing noise. Early 19c. *Midlands and N. England.*

SWANKLE. To sound as a liquid in a half-filled receptacle. Late 19c. *Shetland.*

SWEE. The sound made by a young bird. Late 19c. *Cornwall.*

SWEET-WILLIAM. The goldfinch, *Carduelis carduelis*; so called from its melodious cry. Late 19c.

SWEI. Noise or din; melody; tinnitus, ringing in the ears. *Middle English.*

SWILKER. To make a noise like water shaken in a barrel. Mid 19c. *N. England.*

SWISHING. A beating administered with a cane at Eton; so

called from the sound of the descending cane. Mid 19C.

SWITTLE. A murmuring sound, as made by a stream. Late 19C. *Shetland.*

SWIR. To whirl about so swiftly as to make a whizzing or hum-ming sound. Late 19C. *Somerset.*

SWORLE. To snarl like a dog. 18C. *Sussex.*

SWUFF. To move with a whiz-zing sound; to whistle or hum in a low key or under the breath. Mid 19C. *Berwicks. and Selkirks.*

T

TABBER. A knock, tap; to beat, as on a drum. Late 19c. *Worcs., Leics. and Staffs.*

TABBERER. The lesser-spotted woodpecker, *Dendrocopus minor*; so called from its drumming. Late 19c. *Leics.*

TABOR-AND-PIPE. A musical instrument consisting of a tabor, or tambourine, and a small pipe. The tabor was suspended from the left arm and beaten with a small stick held in the right hand, the pipe held to the mouth and fingered with the left hand. Mid 19c. *Worcs.*

TAGHAIRM. Divination formerly used by the Highlanders of listening to the noise of waterfalls whilst wrapped up in the skin of a newly-slain bullock. Early 19c. *N. Scotland.*

TAISCH. The sound of the voice of a person about to die, heard by someone at a distance beyond the range of ordinary sounds; a form of clairaudience. 18c. *Scotland.*

TALKING. The sound made by a dragging anchor, conveyed to the surface through vibrations in the chain. Early 20c.

TALKING-BUSH. A holly-bush which is fastened to the masthead of ship when in harbour on Christmas Eve; so called because ships and boats are said to talk together on this day. Late 19c. *Cornwall.*

TALK-THIN. To talk in a low voice. Late 19C. *Sussex.*

TALKING-TRUMPET. A child's toy contrived from a small pipe, the larger end of which projects through two halves of an orange skin forming hemispherical cups, partially sewn together. The suggestion of a face is made by fastening two black beans for eyes and a peanut for a nose. By blowing the horn whilst manipulating the 'mouth' of the orange skin, the trumpet talks and says 'mama' quite plainly. Late 19C.

TANG. To ring or toll a bell; to sound loudly, clearly, with a measured sound; especially used of a harsh bell. Early 19C.

TANG-RANG. A noise; an uproar, especially used of the noise formerly made when bees were swarming by beating on shovels. Mid 19C. *Warwicks.*

TANK. To hit a stone against a basin so as to attract attention; to make a ringing noise by striking anything together. Late 19C. *Worcs.*

TANKER. To make a noise. Late 19C. *Derbys.*

TANRACKET. A racket, noise, confusion; a noisy crowd. Late 19C. *Devon.*

TANTARA. A noise; a disturbance; an outcry. Late 19C. *Devon and Cornwall.*

TANTWIVY. The sound of the hunting horn, or that of the post horn. Early 19C.

TASK. The ghost or spirit of a dying person, alleged to call out in repetition of their cries and moans. Mid 19C. *Ross.*

TEET. The smallest sound; the least word. Late 19C. *Banffs.*

TEETLIN. The meadow pipit,

Anthus pratensis; so called in imitation of its twittering note. Late 19c. *Caithness.*

TEEWHEEP. The lapwing or peewit, *Vanellus vanellus*; so called from the sound it utters. Early 19c. *Orkney.*

TE-HE. The sound of a giggle. *Middle English.*

TERPODION. An organ-like instrument in which sonorous wooden or glass rods produce tones when submitted to the friction of a wet ribbon or sound-band, kept in continual motion. Early 19c.

TEUK. The redshank, *Tringa totanus*; so called from its loud and piercing alarm cry. Late 19c. *Norfolk, Essex and Kent.*

TCHOU. An ancient Chinese instrument of percussion constructed of boards about three-quarters of an inch in thickness. In the middle of one of the sides was an aperture into which the hand was passed for the purpose of holding the handle of a wooden hammer, the end of which entered into a hole situated in the bottom of the tchou. The handle was kept in its place by a wooden pin, on which it moved right and left when the instrument was struck with the hammer. 19c.

THAIRM. To play on a stringed instrument. Mid 19c. *Dumfries.*

THOR. A thundering noise. Late 19c. *Yorks.*

THRAMHURN. A trombone. Early 20c. *Isle of Man.*

THROUGH. A 'shouting spell' in a church meeting, consisting of ungovernable shouting, ecstasy, bodily contortions, &c. Early 20c. *United States.*

THREE-THRUMS. The purring sound made by a cat. Also called 'grey thrums'. Early 19c. *Yorks. and Northum.*

THUDDER. A heavy shock or

thud which is accompanied by a loud noise. Late 19C. *Cheshire and Lancs.*

THUNDER-BRATTLE. The noise of thunder-claps following one another in quick succession. Late 19C. *Yorks.*

THUNDER-BUG. A midge; so called from some dim superstition that to kill one induces thunder. Late 19C. *Kent and Sussex.*

THUNDER-CART. A theatrical contrivance for creating the effect of thunder, consisting of a small wooden cart mounted on wheels of an octagonal or serrated shape. The cart contains several large stones or iron cannonballs resting on an iron sheet for a base. A loud rumbling sound may by produced by pushing the cart to and fro back stage. Late 19C.

THUNDER-RUN. A series of inclined wooden channels or gutters in a theatre down which iron or wooden cannon-balls are set rolling to produce a noise suggestive of thunder. The cannon-balls are released from a pen jocularly named the 'rabbit hutch', and may continue along the channels some considerable distance about the theatre, descending by as much as twenty feet. Late 19C.

THUNDER-SPELL. A flat piece of wood like a rule, or an ox's rib notched on the edges and fastened at one end to a string by means of which it is whirled swiftly round the head, and produces a sound which boys call thunder. 18C. *Antrim.*

THUNDERSTONES. Strange objects believed to have been hurled to earth and embedded in the ground following an unusually loud thunderclap. Often these were found to be fossil ammonites or certain mineral deposits, such as quartz crystals. 17C.

THUNGE. A loud and hollow sound; the report of a gun, or of a loud peal of thunder. Mid 19c. *N. England.*

TICKYTAW. The name given to the singers and musicians accompanying dancing girls; so called from the two words *ticky* and *taw* which they continually repeat and chant with great vehemence. Late 19c. *Anglo-Indian.*

TIDDY. Very softly, with very little noise. Late 19c. *Berks.*

TIETICK. The meadow pipit, *Anthus pratensis*; so called in imitation of its short and feeble note. Late 19c. *Shetland.*

TIMBER-TUNED. Having no ear for music; unmusical; having a harsh, unmusical voice. Early 19c. *Scotland.*

TIN-CRY. The peculiar creaking noise made when a bar of tin is bent. It is produced by the grating of the crystal granules on each other. Late 19c.

TIN-EAR. To eavesdrop; to listen with especial care. Early 20c. *United States.*

TIN-KETTLE. To punish a notorious offender by means of 'rough music'; that is, the beating of tin-kettles, &c. Late 19c. *Hants.*

TINNINGE. A ringing of the ears; a reverberating sound. *Middle English.*

TING. To make a ringing noise when bees swarm, by beating a shovel or warming-pan with a key. Late 19C. E. Anglia.

TING-CLIN. A child's imitation of a bell, used upon the occasion of the school-bell ringing: 'Ting-clin, all in', or 'It's ommast ting-clin now', one child will say to another during the play half-hour in the school yard. Mid 19c. *Yorks.*

TING-TANG. A small bell, especially the smallest bell of a

church peal; an unmelodious bell. Late 19C.

TINK-TANK. A term used to express the sound of anything jingling, as of milk falling into a tin pail. Late 19C. *Shetland.*

TINKER. A small church bell, the bell rung just before the service begins. Late 19C. *Berks.*

TINKLE-SWEETIE. The name given to the bell formerly rung at eight o'clock in Edinburgh. Early 19C.

TINKLING-BOX. A slang expression for a pianoforte. Late 19C. *Lancs.*

TINNITENT. Emitting a clear sound. 19C.

TINTAMARRE. A hideous or confused noise; an uproar. 16C.

TIP-TONGUED. To talk in an affectedly refined manner. Late 19C. *Kent and Sussex.*

TIRL. To make a rattling or clattering sound by shaking; to make a tearing sound. Early 19C. *N. England and Scotland.*

TIRLING-PIN. A notched iron door-handle, on which a loose iron ring was hung. Instead of rousing the house with a knock, the caller grated the ring up and down the notches of handle, and produced the sound from which the apparatus took its name. Late 19C. *Scotland and Northum.*

TIRL-GRIND. A turnstile, a revolving gate. Late 19C. *Shetland.*

TIRRA-LIRRA. A verbal imitation of a musical sound, as of the note of a lark or a horn. 17C.

TISHUMS. A fit of sneezing. Late 19C. *Somerset.*

TISSICK. A cough, especially dry, tickling cough; a hacking cough. 16C.

TISSY-WISSY. A dry, tickling cough. Late 19C. *Cornwall.*

TITHERUP. A hand-gallop; so called in imitation of the sound of the horse's footfalls striking the ground in a three-beat pattern. Late 19C. *Lancs.*

TITTEREL. The whimbrel, *Numenius phaeocops*; so called in imitation of its peculiar call. Late 19C. *Sussex.*

TIZZICKY. Wheezy; asthmatic. Early 20C. *United States.*

TODINEN. To be filled with noise, to resound. *Middle English.*

TOKO-FOR-YAM. An old naval expression for crying out before being hurt; borrowed from the negroes. 19C.

TOLLING. The sound made by bees before they swarm. 18C. *Scotland.*

TOMMY-PIPES. A boatswain; so called because he pipes or whistles all hands. Early 20C.

TONG. To sound a bell. Late 19C. *Gloucs.*

TONITRUONE. A percussive instrument which imitates the noise of thunder, consisting of a piece of iron which is fastened to a wooden frame and shaken by hand. Early 20C.

TOPSAIL-YARD-VOICE. A naval officer's voice that is loud and capable of being heard at considerable distance. Technically known as 'power of command'. Early 20C.

TOONEY. To play on a musical instrument; to play tunes. Late 19C. *Cornwall.*

TOOTER. A horn; a trumpet; a tin or wooden whistle. Late 19C. *Fife and Aberdeens.*

TOOTLE. Of a baby: to crow and attempt to talk. Late 19C. *Northants.*

TOOT-MOOT. A low, muttered conversation which begins a row; a dispute. Mid 19C. *N. Scotland.*

TOOTY. To cry in a low, broken voice. Late 19C. *Dorset.*

TOO-ZOO. The ring-dove or wood-pigeon, *Columba palumbus*; so called from its cooing note. Late 19C. *Gloucs.*

TOP. The signal among tailors and sempstresses for snuffing the candle. One cries 'Top', and all the others follow; he who last pronounces the word has to snuff the candle. Mid 19c.

TOPOPHONE. A double ear trumpet for estimating the direction from which sounds proceed, especially for the use of navigators. Late 19c.

TOUSE, TOWSE. To make a noise; a loud disturbance. Hence 'Towser', a name for a dog. Early 19c. *Devon.*

TOWN-AND-GOWN. The fight which used to come off every Fifth of November between the students and the 'cads'. The sides used to shout respectively 'Town!' and 'Gown!' as war-cries. 19c. *Oxfords.*

TOYS. The changes in the song of the linnet, *Carduelis cannabina*, which are fancifully distinguished as the rattle, the laugh, &c. Mid 19c. *London.*

TRANGDILLO. The twanging sound of a stringed musical instrument. 18c.

TREE-SQUEAK. An imaginary bird to which the noise made by trees is attributed by lumberjacks. Early 20c. *United States.*

TREGEAGLE. An apparition said to be the unresting spirit of a wicked magistrate and whose nocturnal wailing is believed to portend storms. 19c. *Cornwall.*

TREMBLING-BELL. A kind of small, hemispherical bell worked by electric currents. A hammer inside the bell is caused to strike by the influence of an electro-magnet. It is often employed on the railways. Mid 19c.

TRIGONON. A harp of the ancient Greeks, with two wooden

pieces, each of about 18 inches in length, constituting its frame. In the course of time a third bar was added to the trigonon to resist the tension of the strings, and then improved improved further when the upper bar was made slightly curved, whereby the instrument obtained greater strength and more elegance of form. 19C.

TRILODEON. A melodeon improved by combining with each key two, three, or more separate reeds so that differences in the touch of the performer may cause different degrees of sound to be given to the same musical note. Mid 19C.

TRIM. To tune an instrument; to 'thrum' or play on a banjo, &c. Late 19C. *Lancs.*

TROAT. To cry as the buck does at rutting-time. 17C.

TROOPING. A habit of Revivalist meetings, where the dancers strive for spiritual possession by breathing with a short sharp intake that sounds like the bark of a dog. If persisted in, this will produce that semiconscious condition which is favourable to the communications of spirits. Early 20C. *Jamaica.*

TROPIE. The noise made by a troop of men. *Middle English.*

TROUNCING. A custom formerly observed at deaths, where the corpse was placed in the coffin as soon as possible, and then at the wake gathering it was carried around the room with unearthly noise and clamour. This was supposed to frighten away evil spirits, and to act magically upon the soul's enemies. 18C. *Pembrokes.*

TROZE. The sound made by the wash of water at the bows of a boat; the sound made by a school of fish when breaking the surface of the water. Late 19C. *Cornwall.*

TRUMPET. To stump or tramp about noisily. Late 19C. *Berks.*

TRUMPET-BUGLE. A wind instrument which combines the properties of the trumpet and bugle. Between the mouth-piece and the tube of the bugle is interposed a tube of brass, a spring valve, and a tuning slide. When the valve is pressed upon and the whole instrument is sounded, it becomes a trumpet. Mid 19C.

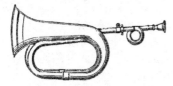

TRUMPET-KEEKS. The hollow stalks of the wild angelica, *Angelica sylvestris*, or some allied plant, which are made by boys into trumpets. Late 19C. *Northum.*

TRUMPETER. A drunkard who possesses the facility of belching and passing wind at the same time. 17C.

TRUNKMAKER-LIKE. Of one who produces more noise than he performs work. Mid 19C.

TUBBY. Resembling a tub; specifically sounding dull and without resonance, like a tub; wanting elasticity of sound; as a tubby violin. Early 19C.

TUCK. Of poultry: to cluck, to make a clucking noise. Mid 19C. *Devon.*

TUCKAHOE. One who speaks with a Southern accent. Mid 19C. *United States.*

TUCKET. A slight flourish on a trumpet; a fanfare. 17C.

TUG-SLUG. To tramp noisily and heavily. Late 19C. *Lincs.*

TULLUNGE. A child's word used to express the sound made by the report of a gun or cannon. Late 19C. *Lancs.*

TUNEABLE. Having an ear for music; able to sing. 16C.

TWANK. To beat or sound, as a stationary steam-engine; to drop a carpenter's chalk-line with a slap. Late 19C. *Yorks. and E. Anglia.*

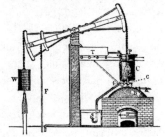

TWANKLE. To twang with the fingers on a musical instrument. Late 19C. *Leics. and Warwicks.*

TWEATLING. Twittering, chirping of birds. Late 19C. *Devon.*

TWEEDLE-DEE. An indifferent musician; a sorry fiddler; a musical sound carelessly made. Early 19C. *Orkney and Scotland.*

TWINK. The chaffinch, *Fringilla coelebs*; so called on account of its sharp, musical, chirpy note. Late 19C. *W. England, Cheshire and Shrops.*

TWINKELINGE. The act of plucking a harp; the sound of a harp. *Middle English.*

TWIRL. A flourish of words; a grace-note in singing. Late 19C. *Caithness and Aberdeens.*

TWITTLE. The sound made by a person's fingers in water. Late 19C. *Shetland.*

TWIT-ME-DICK. The quail, *Coturnix communis*; so called from its chirping and 'twitting'. Late 19C. *Oxfords.*

TYSTIE. The black guillemot, *Cepphus grylle*; so called in imitation of its cry. Mid 19C. *Orkney.*

U

UIB. To make a moaning and melancholy sound. Late 19C. *Shetland.*

UMBLE. A choking sound made in the throat of a cow. Late 19C. *Shetland.*

UNCLE-DUDLEY. The person speaking, especially at a meeting or lecture. Early 20C. *United States.*

UP-SPIRITS. The daily pipe on board ship which sends to the duty ratings to draw the exact amount of rum for the issue at mid-day. Early 20C.

UTICK. The whinchat, *Saxicola rubetra*; so called from its constant cry which resembles 'u-teek, u-teek'. Late 19C. *Notts.*

UTIS. A riotous and noisy assembly; confusion, din; such as used to accompany the eighth day of a festival. Late 19C. *Worcs.*

V

VACAYA. Any mechanical device built for the reproduction of sound, such as a phonograph or gramophone player. Early 20c. *Polari.*

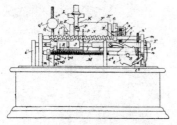

VAMP. To accompany a singer by ear; to improvise or play on a musical instrument. 18c.

VENOUS-HUM. A humming sound, or bruit, heard during auscultation of the veins of the neck in anaemia. Mid 19c.

VESICULAR-MURMUR. The sound, audible on auscultation of the chest, made by the air entering and leaving the air vesicles of the lungs in respiration. Late 19c.

VISSIK. A song or ballad accompanying a dance, the time being kept by the feet without need for any musical instrument. Early 19c. *Shetland.*

VOCHE. A voice; a singer. Early 20c. *Polari.*

VOCULE. A slight sound of the voice, as occurs at the end of certain consonants. Early 19c.

W

WAFF. To bark or yelp as a puppy or small dog; to make the sound of puffing. 18c. *N. England.*

WAGGA-POT. A bell hung from the neck of a bullock. Early 20c. *Australia.*

WAITS. Musicians of the lower order, who in most towns play under the windows of the chief inhabitants at midnight, a short time before Christmas, for which they collect a christmas-box from house to house. They are said to derive their name of waits from being always in waiting to celebrate weddings and other joyous events happening within their district. Early 19c.

WAKERELL-BELL. A bell for calling people in the morning. Mid 19c. *Kent.*

WAKE-WAILERS. Professional mourners who are hired for funerals. Late 19c. *Yorks.*

WALLOP. To move rapidly with a gurgling or rattling noise; the noise of boiling broth or porridge. Early 19C. *Scotland and Northum.*

WARBLE. To play the quicker notes of a piece of bagpipe music, in which there are a large number of grace notes. Late 19C. *Argyll.*

WARBLETON-SKULLS. A pair of skulls kept until recent times in Warbleton Priory. They were believed to be those of a former owner and his murderer, and ghastly nocturnal noises followed any attempt to move them. Late 19C. *Sussex.*

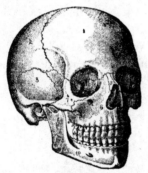

WARN. Of a clock: to make a clicking sound immediately before striking the hour. Late 19C. *Stirlings., Ayrshire and Northum.*

WARNING. A sound taken as a portent or death-omen, such as the howl of a dog, the ticking of the death watch, or some mysterious knock. Late 19C. *Scotland.*

WASSLE. To make a rattling or hoarse sound in breathing. Late 19C. *N. Ireland.*

WATER-GUNS. Sounds of gunshots said to be heard around the shores of Lough Neagh and by persons sailing on the lake. The cause of the sounds, which are generally heard in calm weather, has not been explained. Late 19C. *N. Ireland.*

WATER-HAMMER. A vessel partly filled with water, exhausted of air, and hermetically sealed. When reversed or shaken the water, being unimpeded by air, strikes the sides with a sound like that of a hammer. 18C.

WAY-GANG. A faint sound; a whisper. Late 19C. *Shetland.*

WEAK. To squeak; to speak or sing in a thin, squeaky voice; to whistle at intervals. Early 19C.

WEDDING-PSALM. If a bride appears at church within a few Sundays after the wedding, it is customary for the singers to sing a particular psalm, thence called the 'wedding-psalm'. At Winston Church the 133rd psalm is selected; in some churches the 128th. Mid 19C. *Co. Durham.*

WEEPER. A lachrymose beggar,

one who cries as he hears his own hard-luck story. Early 20C. *United States.*

WERBLANDE. Of the wind: blowing shrilly, whistling. *Middle English.*

WERBLEN. Of a trumpet: to sound, especially in battle. *Middle English.*

WETHER-BLEAT. The snipe, *Gallinago gallinago*; so called from its peculiar cry resembling the bleat of a sheep. Late 19C. *Aberdeens.*

WET-BIRD. The chaffinch, *Fringilla coelebs*; so called because its 'weet weet' cry is considered to foretell to rain. Late 19C. *Rutland.*

WET-MY-FOOT. The quail, *Coturnix coturnix*; so called in imitation of its cry. Late 19C. *N. Ireland.*

WHANGING. A beating, usually one of such severity as to be widely heard. Late 19C. *Yorks.*

WHASSL-WHIEZL. To wheeze in breathing. Late 19C. *Shetland and Orkney.*

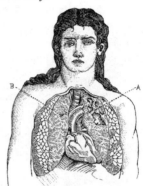

WHAUP. To cry as a curlew; the noise made by a chick when it has lost its mother. Late 19C. *Cumber.*

WHEEBERT. To whistle. Late 19C. *Aberdeens.*

WHEEL. To shout a challenge to fight. Late 19C. *Ireland.*

WHEEL-BIRD. The nightjar, *Caprimulgus europaeus*; so called from the strange whirring, jarring noise, something like that made by a spinning-wheel, uttered by the bird on summer evenings. Late 19C. *Stirlings.*

WHEEP. To produce a sharp sound; to squeak; the sound

made by a sword or dagger when drawn swiftly from its sheath. Late 19c. *Scotland and Ireland.*

WHEEPLE. A lacklustre and ineffectual attempt of a person to whistle loudly. Late 19c. *Scotland.*

WHEETIE. A call made to summon poultry, especially ducks; the peeping or twittering of young birds. 17c. *N. Scotland.*

WHEEZER. A phonograph. Late 19c.

WHEEZIE. Of a fire: to blaze with a hissing noise. Late 19c. *Lanarks. and Clydes.*

WHEW. To whistle with a shrill pipe, like a plover; a mill-whistle to summon the workpeople to their labour; the noise of whistling heard in houses which are unsound in the wind. Early 19c. *Scotland and N. England.*

WHEW-DUCK. The wigeon, *Anas penelope*; so called from its peculiar whistling call-note. Late 19c. *Yorks.*

WHEWL. To whistle softly; to twitter, as a young bird beginning to sing. Mid 19c. *Lincs.*

WHIEW. The noise made in driving hogs. 18c. *Kent.*

WHIFFLE. A shrill intermittent note, with little variation of tone. Late 19c. *Scotland.*

WHIFFLER. One who plays the fife or flute; one who goes at the head of a procession to clear the way for it by continually waving a sword of lath or latten, making a 'whiffing' sound in the air. 17c. *Scotland, Lancs. and E. Anglia.*

WHILK. To howl like a dog; to mutter to oneself. 18c. *Sussex.*

WHILLALOO. An outcry; a hubbub, commotion; a prolonged strain of melancholy music. 17c.

WHINDLE. A low cry. Early 19c.

WHINK. The peculiar short yelp a dog gives when close to its game; the suppressed bark of a shepherd's dog when, from want of breath, he is unable to extend his cry. Early 19c. *Selkirks. and Northum.*

WHINNOCK. To whimper; to sob; to whine as a dog. Late 19c. *N. England.*

WHINTIN. A dark-coloured slate found in Skiddaw. When struck it gives out sounds, and the celebrated 'musical stones' are made of it. Early 19c. *Cumber.*

WHISPERER. An evil spirit alleged to creep up behind unsuspecting persons in daytime, softly imploring them to turn their heads but for one moment. Any one so doing would have their neck broken instantly by the Whisperer. Late 19c. *Lancs.*

WHISPERING-BARITONE. Railwaymen's slang for a loud-voiced, noisy character. Early 20c.

WHISPERING-PUDDING. A sort of plum-pudding in which the plums are very close together, and so are jocularly claimed to be able to converse by whispering. Late 19c. *Warwicks and Northants.*

WHIST. Not speaking; not making a noise; silent. 16c.

WHISTLE-BINKIE. A musician who plays at penny-weddings and other social gatherings, and trusts for his remuneration to the generosity of the party. Late 19c. *Scotland.*

WHISTLE-CUP. A drinking cup with a whistle attached: the last toper capable of using the whistle received the cup as a prize. 19c.

WHISTLE-KIRK. A church with an organ in it; an Episcopalian church. Late 19c. *Scotland.*

WHISTLE-WEED. A kind of brown bladder-bearing seaweed;

so called along the lower banks of the Severn because whistles are made from it. Late 19C. *Gloucs.*

WHISTLER. Chance labourer at the docks; from the poor fellow whistling for work. Late 19C. *London.*

WHISTLING-BILLY. A steam locomotive. Early 20C. *United States.*

WHISTLING-DICK. The song-thrush, *Turdus musicus.* Late 19C. *S. England.*

WHISTLING-DOVYER. The golden plover, *Charadrius pluvialis.* Late 19C. *Berks.*

WHISTLING-MATCH. A rustic contest in which a prize is conferred upon the whistler who can whistle clearest, and go through his tune while a clown, or a merry-andrew, makes laughable grimaces before him. Late 19C.

WHISTLING-SHOP. A beer-house, where it was the fashion for customers to whistle for their drink. Late 19C. *Lancs.*

WHISTLING-TEAL. A duck of the species *Dendrocygna awsuree*; so called from its loud wheezing call. A numerous flock of these whistlers is sometimes seen in Bengal sitting in a tree, a curious habit for ducks. Late 19C. *Anglo-Indian.*

WHIT. To play on the flute; to tootle. Late 19C. *Wales.*

WHIT-AND-DUB. A musical instrument resembling the pipe and tabor of Scripture. Mid 19C. *Berks.*

WHITE-POWDER. A noiseless gunpowder, popularly supposed to be used by poachers. 17C.

WHITHERING. The noise as of people lumbering up and down stairs. Late 19C. *Yorks.*

WHITTER. A low, plaintive, murmuring noise; the mournful, single note uttered by a bird. Late 19C. *Northum. and Berks.*

WHOOPER-UPS. Inferior, noisy singers. Late 19C. *Theatrical slang.*

WHOOPING-BOY. A 'duppy' or

ghostly apparition which rides a three-footed horse, having one front leg and two rear legs. The ghost whoops like a human being and dances among the trees in the woods. Early 20c. *Jamaica.*

WHOOP-UP. To put a musical instrument into tune. Late 19c. *United States.*

WILLY-LILT. To produce a cry like that of the common sandpiper, *Actitis hypoleucos.* Mid 19c. *Cumber.*

WILLY-WAMBLES. A complaint of the bowels attended with a rumbling noise. 18c. *Scotland.*

WILLY-WICKET. The common sandpiper, *Actitis hypoleucos*; so called from the piping note this bird utters when disturbed. Late 19c. *N. England.*

WIND-CLAPPER. A wooden contrivance instrument erected in fields for scaring birds. Late 19c. *Devon.*

WINDOW-RATTLER. A person who snores loudly. Early 20c. *United States.*

WINNOW. The sound made by a horse when wishing for food or water. Late 19c. *Herefs.*

WISHIE. Not the slightest sound; profound silence. Mid 19c. *Fife.*

WISHING-COW. A cow through which a supernatural being works its malign magic, said to cause the death of a person by lowing repeatedly at night. Early 20c. *Jamaica.*

WIZZEN. To whine, as a dog; to bellow; to make a noise. Early 19c. *N. England.*

WOFFLE. Of a musician: to manipulate, mask or evade a note, or even a difficult passage. Late 19c.

WOODIN-UP. To applaud by stamping the feet with gusto. Early 20c. *United States.*

WOOD-NOTE. A wild musical note, like that of a songbird. 17c.

WOODPECKER. Military slang for a machine-gun, from the rapid sound of its firing. Late 19C. *Australia and United States.*

WOOMER. A humming-board; a child's toy made of a closely-notched lath attached at one end to a string, and making a loud humming noise when whirled around at arm's length. Late 19C. *Isle of Man.*

WOUKER. A dog that is greatly addicted to barking. Late 19C. *Northants.*

Wow. To make a loud mewing noise, as cats sometimes do. Late 19C. *Lincs.*

WRAITH-BELL. A bell supposed to sound before a death. Late 19C. *Wigtowns.*

WULVE. Of a bell: to ring. Late 19C. *Devon.*

WUTHER. Of the wind: to rage, bluster; of cattle: to bellow. Mid 19C. *N. England.*

Y

YACKLE. The green woodpecker, *Gecinus viridus*; so called from its loud, shrill laugh. Late 19c. *Somerset and Herefords.*

YAFFLE. To bark; to yelp; to yap, as a little dog; to talk as if toothless or mumbingly. Late 19c. *Midlands and N. England.*

YAG. To make a noise; to talk angrily; to quarrel. Late 19c. *Shetland and Orkney.*

YALDER. The noisy and rapid barking of a dog, especially when in pursuit of prey, or when bringing an animal to bay. Late 19c. *Scotland and Yorks.*

YALLACRACK. A loud outcry; a great noise of voices. Late 19c. *Shetland.*

YAM. To eat greedily and with the attendant noise that usually accompanies voracious feeding; the noise made in so eating. Late 19c. *Lincs. and Yorks.*

YAMMER-YOUL. A bell in the Paisley Wee Steeple; so called for being always rung when a burial was passing. Mid 19c. *Renfrews.*

YAMPH. To bark; to yelp; to yap, as a small dog. 18c. *Scotland and Northum.*

YARL. To bawl; to utter a loud and discordant sound; the discordant noises of poultry. Late 19c. *Notts. and Essex.*

YARM. A discordant, disagreeable sound; to cry as a wild beast. Late 19c. *Yorks. and Lincs.*

YAUP. To shout, bawl, cry aloud; to talk in a loud, boisterous manner. Late 19c. *N. England and Scotland.*

YELLOW-RATTLE. The herbaceous annual, *Rhinanthus minor*; so called from its fruit, which contains loose, rattling seeds. 16c.

YELP. To sing in chorus; in all music halls the audiences join in the choruses. Late 19c.

YELPER. An animal that makes a yelping noise; the avocet, *Recurvirostra avosetta*; so called from its sharp, shrill cry. 18c. *Lincs.*

YERR. To yell, shout out. Late 19c. *Devon.*

YETH-HOUNDS. Dogs without heads, supposed to be the unembodied or transmigrated souls of unbaptized children, which roam the woods at night, making a wailing noise. Mid 19c. *Somerset, Devon and Cornwall.*

YIKE. The call of the woodpecker. Late 19c. *Surrey and Hants.*

YIKKA. To snarl, as a dog. Late 19c. *Shetland.*

YIP. A dog, especially a small, nervous animal who 'yips' or barks in a shrill way. Early 20c. *United States.*

YOFFLE. To eat or drink greedily, so as to make a noise. Late 19c. *Kent.*

YOICKS. A cry of following during the chase. Late 19c. *Dorset.*

YOKES. Hiccups. Late 19C. *Somerset*.

YOLLER. To bellow; to yell discordantly; to speak indistinctly through passion. Late 19C. *Lakeland, Roxburghs. and Northum.*

YOPPER. An excessively talkative person. Early 20C. *Somerset*.

YOPPING. The noise made by a dog in full cry after game, or when baying a stranger. Late 19C. *Gloucs*.

YOOP. A word imitative of a sobbing sound. Mid 19C.

YOTL. Diminutive bells made of copper or other sonorous metal by the Aztecs and strung together to make clusters. 19C.

YOTTENING. The noise made in the throat by swallowing a large mouthful of liquid. Late 19C. *Yorks*.

YOWPER. A street-crier. Late 19C. *Yorks*.

Z

Zamomba. A simple Spanish musical instrument made from a wide-mouthed jar over which is stretched a piece of parchment. A stick is then inserted through a hole in the parchment and rubbed with the fingers to produce a curious sound. 19c.

Ziph language. A way of disguising English in use among the boys at Winchester College, and communicated to newcomers for the fee of half a guinea. The secret is to repeat the vowel or diphthong of every syllable, prefixing to the vowel so repeated the letter 'G', and placing the accent on the intercalated syllable. Thus, for example, 'Shall we go away in an hour?' becomes 'Shagall wege gogo agawagay igin hougour?' The language of Ziph is far inferior to any of the slangs of the lower orders. Late 19c.

GAZETTEER

ENGLAND

BERKSHIRE. Chackling, clumput, crick, hocksing, jingling-match, low-bell, May-horn, nutter, pee-wit, pobble, quelch, querk, rucketting, screech-hawk, scrump, slippetin, snapper, squatch, tiddy, tinker, trumpet, whistling-dovyer, whit-and-dub, whitter.

BUCKINGHAMSHIRE. Bull-rattle.

CHESHIRE. Barst, bawk, cherry-clack, chuckling, cocky-keeko, hammer-and-tongs, kerry, May-singers, ninny-neeno, plunder, rackapelt, ran-tan, rick, ricking-ripe, runt, rute, solch, soo, souling, thudder, twink.

CLEVELAND. Bree, cry-up.

CORNWALL. Bal, balk, bucca, caprouse, chauk, clacker, cockathodon, conk, coopers, craky, crowdy-crawn, cuckold, curwillet, Dando's-dogs, dido, drilsy, garm, gow, hewer, hoolybuss, hubbadalion, knockers, May-music, morbleu, murre, nuggie, passon, randivoose, rounge, rucksel, scat, scavel-an-gow, shallal, skerry-kabberish, slatter-cum-drash, sligerin, sniffer, spurre, swee, talking-bush, tantara, tissy-wissy, tooney, tregeagle, troze, yeth-hounds.

COUNTY DURHAM. Blowing-for-burns, bouk, caleveering, coffin, crune, dark, darking-dog, grune, jowl, ower-tune, rift, sap-whistle, sisserara, skrike, wedding-psalm.

CUMBERLAND. Bolder, chitter-waow, click-reel, crune, dark, dreen, dreep, golder, hisk, jeyk, mean, mewtle, natter, nattler, peuk, plit-plat, rattle-can, rounge, slobber, whaup, whintin, willy-lilt.

DERBYSHIRE. Chink, chuckle, skirlcock, squirrel-hunting, tanker.

DORSET. Bell-plow, bird-clacker, bleare, chatter-mag, chimcheay, hobble, home-screech, keepen, larry, lowsen, morbleu, murre, noises, plounce, pop, snapping-tongs, snoach, snock, snorter, squeapity, squit, toot-moot, yoicks.

EAST ANGLIA. Bear-a-parl, bell-soller, bottle-bump, bull's-noon, bumble, buzzard, churchman, clapper-board, clapping-table, crow-keeper, dullor, dutter, ear-bell, fizmer, galder, gobble, gruffle, hedge-accentor, hummer, julk, lowder, luller, lure, mag, mewsing, mob, mork-shriek, muck-spout, mush, pitter, plounce, prate, quackle, rasp, rattock, ring-awk, sanny, shawm, shrieker, snicker, soul-bell, squat, ting, twank, whiffler.

ENGLISH GYPSY. Bosh, boshero, boshomengro, caller, cor, crambrookos, gill, gilly, gillyaws, godli, jibb, mi-dooveelesko-godli, nautering, nobbings, nucker, poshavaben, rill, rocker, rockeropen, shelengro, shindy, sholl.

ESSEX. Aunt, clanjandering, duvver, gleaning-bell, grizzle, harvest-horn, husk, jink, keeping-Dovercourt, quackle, rootle, scrame, teuk, yarl.

GLOUCESTERSHIRE. Bandore, chackle, cooter, crank-bird, doppet, dream-hole, gawk, gibberwoling, hazen, hick-wall, pretty-pretty-creature, screech-drosle, tong, too-zoo, whistle-weed, yopping.

HAMPSHIRE. Badger's-band, bleating, chatter, clinkers, clocking, colt-pixy, cowowing, crink-to-crank, dumbledore, glox, jar-bird, louster, louster-crown, lurry, pop, slut, tin-kettle, yike.

HEREFORDSHIRE. Hobbing, singing-bird, winnow.

KENT. Bop, cluther, cock-bell, gross, herring-piece, hicket, hodening, hussle, hyste, knucker, lerry, nang, peety, rookery, scrooch, sizzing, squashle, teuk, thunder-bug, tip-tongued, wakerell-bell, whiew, yoffle.

LAKELAND. Losh, skroke, soddering, soom, yoller.

LANCASHIRE. Bark, bell-tinker, buzzard, chink-cough, click-me-toad, clit-clat, drum, flusk, gabbleratchet, huzzer, maulp, mutes, neeze, piping, quicken-whistle, ran-tan, rattle-can, reek, rick, solch, soo, souling, speawker, striker, thudder, tinkling-box, titherup, trim, tullunge, whiffler, whisperer, whistling-shop.

LEICESTERSHIRE. Hog, sing-rovings, soom, squilker, tabber, tabberer, twankle.

LINCOLNSHIRE. Channer, chickering, click-up, clocks, cluck, flop, gig, growze, hoin, jaup, keck, meadowcrake-cutbox, nacker, rackapelt, saum, scolding-wife, sissing-medicine, skreel, slarg, slammock, spur-peal, struncheon, tug-slug, whewl, wow, yam, yarm, yelper.

LONDON. Agitator, Barking-Creek, barrikin, bawler, beef-heart, bible-mill, billingsgate, box-of-toys, bread-and-cheese, breeze, call, canary, carts, catgut-scrapers, chanter, chanting-ken, chaunter-culls, chirrup, constant-screamer, crack-the-monica, death-hunter, fourteen-hundred, free-and-easy, griddler, half-a-pint-of-mild-and-bitter, harry's-worrier, hi-diddle-diddle, hinchinarfer, hummums, invisible-girl, joanna, marrowskying, molly-o'morgan, mump, music-duffer, patterers, patter-flash, public-patterers, rabbit-and-pork, ringing-in, schlemozzle, shoe-leather, slum, stewed-prune, toys, whistler.

MIDLANDS. Bolch, charm, chat, chelp, crowp, muff, peak, peggy-cutthroat, pither, sleep, squean, suther, yaffle.

NORFOLK. Dippurl, heck, hish, hisser, lamb, rattle-wings, reel, scape, scissor-grinder, smack, teuk.

NORTH OF ENGLAND. Babble, beal, bee-baw, belder, blether-baise, bolch, brabblement, brattle, cawdy-mawdy, chang, cheeper, chelp, churr, cluntering, crake, crank, crean, croakum-shire, cronk, croupy-craw, crowp, dead-chack, diddle, drate, dumb-cake, frap, Gabriel's-hounds, gewgaw, goul, greet, hacker, hask, hoo-roo, horse's-leg, howch, hummer, huzz, kevel, kink, kittle-up, knack, knack-and-rattle, ledden, lill, loal, maddle, mag, munging, nattle, pegh, prate, raising, rasper, ream, rout, shirl, singing-hinny, siss, sleep, slorp, snirt, steven, stound, stramash, suther, swilker, thunge, tirl, waff, whew, whinnock, willy-wicket, wizzen, wuther, yaffle, yaup.

NORTHAMPTONSHIRE. Chickering, cramp, death-coach, frizzling, gawthrush, glink, jar-peg, mouse, pig's-whisper, pinkety, purring, row-dow, squean, tootle, whispering-pudding, wouker.

NORTHUMBERLAND. Birr, bouk, brag, cockling, crowdy-main, dunder, fothering-horn, golder, groonge, grozer-squeals, grumpher, gurl, hirdy-girdy, jowling, knackers, piper, puist, raird, ramp, rat-rhyme, reeshle, rounge, sea-roarer, shork, skreel, slughorn, snook, sob, three-thrums, tirling-pin, trumpet-keeks, wallop, warn, whink, whitter, yamph, yoller.

NOTTINGHAMSHIRE. Chink, growze, scrannel-piping, slop, soam, squilker, utick, yarl.

OXFORDSHIRE. Curvew-bell, hocksing, nutter, quick-me-dick, quobble, squatch, town-and-gown, twit-me-dick.

RUTLAND. Wet-bird.

SCILLY ISLES. Cockathodon.

SHROPSHIRE. Belownder, caim, chink-chink, churching-mice, clary, cuckoo-foot-ale, hoost, jack-squealer, kerry, latitat, neeze, pump-borer, shredcock, souling, twink.

SOMERSET. Belg, bim-boms, bladder-mouth, charm-birds, chatter-pie, cheese-bird, chipper, crink-to-crank, crowdy-kit, gurds, haffer, happen, homany, home-screech, humdrum, latitat, lidden, mapse, mouse-snap, panker, pop, quest, scape, scour, snack, snoach, speak, squacket, strim-strum, swir, tishums, yeth-hounds, yokes, yopper.

SOUTH OF ENGLAND. Charm, chat, chavish, churchman, clacket, humstrum, rouser, whistling-dick.

STAFFORDSHIRE. Bell-tinker, caim, guggle, tabber.

SUFFOLK. Cruckle, frank, grill, hammergag, harmony, jill-hooter, laist, laistly, scissor-grinder.

SURREY. Cluck-hen, cocket, hicket, knucker, scape, sizzing, squacket, yike.

SUSSEX. Bawl, burn-whispering, clapper, galley-bird, grout-headed, horn-fair, howlers, knabbler, knucker, louster, lurry, mum-chance, nang, narre, ollering-owl, parly, rake, rookery, Shipley-echo, sizzing, skreel, slosh, squacket, sworle, talk-thin, thunder-bug, tip-tongued, titterel, Warbleton-skulls, whilk.

WARWICKSHIRE. Clicketing, guggle, hish, humbering, lip, scrump, tang-rang, twankle, whispering-pudding.

WEST COUNTRY. Clacket, crap, cronk, drane, dumbledore, hawch, hiren, hooi, hoost, huffle, humbuzz, humstrum, nang, querk, scroop, skimmington, stram, twink.

WESTMORELAND. Blodder, hisk, jercock, losh, mewtle, slatter, soom.

WILTSHIRE. Bellock, cawk, dutter, glox, hackle, hazen, hocksing, lottle, mouse, rumpum-scrumpum, screech-devil, scrupetty, shandy-foo, singeration, strim-strum.

WORCESTERSHIRE. Chackle, chuckle, churchman, cow-mouthed, fidther, hooting, pack-racket, reach, rolly, splother, tabber, tabor-and-pipe, tank, utis

YORKSHIRE. Baff, Bainbridge-horn, bander, barguest, bawther, belch, bell-hoss, bell-tinker, blether, bolder, bottle-bump, bragging, bumbass, cake, censioner, chaffle, cheet, cheeter, chissup, chuttering, clap-a-benny, clap-cans, clavver, clicket, creak-warner, cuttering, dark, darking-dog, death-warner, derrum, devil-screamer, devil's-knell, drane-poke, dream-hole, fiddle-father, fiddle-grass, flusk, gabbleratchet, gecken, gig, gizzened, han, hear, hedge-creep, heeze, hick-haw, jaup, jingling-johnnie, keck, kinkin-coff, knackers, lalling, lolder, muff, neeze, neezle, nitter, pad-foot, pech, piping, play-pipes, rackapelt, rap-tapping, reasty-cropped, reek, rick, rift, rimple, Ripon-horn, roupy-weather, rumbler, scallibrat, scrate, scrive, scrunt, shill, skeldering, skrike, skrurk, sledge, snavel, sob, soo, staupings, thor, three-thrums, thunder-brattle, ting-clin, twank, wake-wailers, whanging, whew-duck, whithering, yalder, yam, yarm, yottening, yowper.

SCOTLAND

GENERAL. Aich, birr, blout, brattle, buck, bummlan, chang, cheeper, cheeps, chirl, churr, clam-shells, clap, clatch, clatter-bone, clatter-stoup, cleiro, clunk, cockieleerie, coronach, correnoy, crake, crank, crood, crooner, crose, dead-bell, diddle, dinling, dirl, dooff, doyst, dring, drizzen, drone, dunder, fire-drum, fuff, gaff, gaw-haw, gew-gaw, golder, gollar, greet, hallyoch, harker, hask, heather-bleat, hirdy-girdy, hirsle, hooch, hoozle, howch, howk-chowk, jorram, jow, kittle-up, knack, knoit, lill, loal, lown, meout, mush, nick, ouff, peak, pegh, peuk, plouter, pout, raird, rash-whish, rasper, rat-rhyme, rattle-bag, ream, reeshle, risk, rookery, roupit, rout, roxle, rumbling-kirn, screech-bird, sea-mew, sirdon, skirl-in-the-pan, slorp, slump, snagger, snirt, steven, stound, stramash, sumphion, taisch, timber-tuned, tirl, tirling-pin, tolling, tweedle-dee, wallop, warning, wheep, wheeple, whew, whiffle, whiffler, whistle-binkie, whistle-kirk, willy-wambles, yalder, yamph, yaup.

NORTH OF SCOTLAND. Chirple, cuddlie, reemish, ruddy, taghairm, toot-moot, wheetie.

SOUTH OF SCOTLAND. Huddy-craw.

WEST OF SCOTLAND. Ruff, squaich.

ABERDEENSHIRE. Almanie-whistle, bleak-bleak, futhir, graig, pipple, plype, scroinoch, sprig, squalloch, stichle, tooter, twirl, wether-bleat, wheebert.

ANGUS. Blocher, clocharet.

AYRSHIRE. Bum-clock, gludder, heather-peep, rave, sob, sottle, splorroch, stock-and-horn, warn.

BANFFSHIRE. Bairge, cheepart, clowk, dead-drap, glag, graig, heemlin, hurl, kae, minneer, plapper, plype, reemle-rammle, scroinoch, skirlie-weeack, sprallich, squalloch, teet.

BERWICKSHIRE. Hurlie-go-thorow, pitcake, swuff.

CAITHNESS. Elf-mill, glumsh, hurl, mourn, skirlag, snorick, squaich, teetlin, twirl.

CLYDESDALE. Gauner, marr, nyuckfit, scrunt, slagger, wheezie.

DUMFRIESSHIRE. Blitter-blatter, chark, ninny-niawing, thairm.

EDINBURGH. Lolaby, tinkle-sweetie.

FIFE. Booff, gorge, kingle-kangle, tooter, wishie.

GALLOWAY. Cur-doo, glouk, hiving-sough, jorgle, jorinker, jumm, jurr, labb, mean, pinkle-pankle, runch.

LOTHIAN. Dead-knock, dead-ruckle, drow, gruzzle, keelie, poor-willie, rumble-tumble.

ORKNEY. Brimtud, buck, creist, dore, drone, glafter, goilbrul, gupp, hanyadu, hurklin, hurless, jaffse, knirk, kreest, lun, nick, peester, pleep, pling, rain-goose, scale, scolder, skroke, snorick, steinkle, teewheep, tweedle-dee, tystie, whassl-whiezl, yag.

PERTHSHIRE. Blocher, fung, jorg, sprig.

RENFREWSHIRE. Blethering-tam, boiled-bell, clappertie-clink, gruzzle, hottle, rattle-shot, stichle, yammer-youl.

ROXBURGHSHIRE. Bule, dead-ruckle, doudle, drool, jimmer, nickerers, saw-sharpener, yoller.

SELKIRKSHIRE. Swuff, whink.

SHETLAND. Brimtud, claag, dore, dunder-clugs, gallafer, glafter, goilbrul, gue, gupp, hanyadu, hurklin, hurless, hush, jaffse, klaag, klurmose, knirk, kreks, kroytl, loadie-grunt, luderhorn, lun, marriage-shake, neesterin, njoag, oob, peester, pikk, pleep, pling, rain-goose, reen, shud, skeyld, skrol, smucksin, snush, snyirk, soitl, spraech, steinkle, su·lk, swankle, swittle, tietick, tink-tank, tirl-grind, twittle, umble, vissick, way-gang, whassl-whiezl, yallacrack, yikka.

STIRLINGSHIRE. Warn, wheel-bird.

WALES

GENERAL. Pibcorn, whit.

NORTH WALES. Knockers.

PEMBROKESHIRE. Lunk, rumpus, shuck-shack, spurre, trouncing.

ISLE OF MAN

Bannag, bazer, billy-yn-tweet, blass, cabbag, carwhillag, cleash, collan-bing, dhonk, gloar, gurragh, howlaa, hushee-bow, kred, quisle, rawl, reezhagh, rip, scanky, sthoo, thramhurn, woomer.

IRELAND

GENERAL. Drizzen, Killarney-echo, meout, pillaloo, wheel, wheep.
NORTHERN IRELAND. Chitterling, hi-how, Peter-Dick, screech-cock, squaich, wassle, water-guns, wet-my-foot.

AUSTRALIA

Bell-sheep, bubbly-mary, bushman's-clock, cooee, four-o'clock, grinder, jingle, laughing-jack, paroo-dog, roaring, shepherd's-harp, shepherd's-whistle, squeaker, wagga-pot, woodpecker.

NEW ZEALAND

Crackee-crackee.

INDIA

Banjee, banyan-fight, bobbery, bobbery-pack, buck-stick, bulbul, collery-horn, galee, gecko, gum-gum, hobson-jobson, phut, tickytaw, whistling-teal.

JAMAICA

Abeng, banda, banter-sing, bender, croaking-lizard, cut-cedar-board, cut-English, drummer, greeting, grunt, gumbi-man, jawbone, jenkoving, johnny-ho, kling-kling, merry-wang, pecheery, purification, qua-bird, rookaw, rumba-box, shell-blow, trooping, whooping-boy, wishing-cow.

UNITED STATES

Angel's-whisper, bagpipe, ballyhoo, bazoo, berlue, blare, bom, boohoo-owl, boomer, bubbler, callithump, canter, catouse, chitter, chug-a-lug, chugger, clabber-mouthed, dee-dee, ding-dong, doodlebug, dummy, ear-string, fowl-crow, gitbox, gosling-patch, griddle, grind, growler, hassle, jar-fly, jook, lumberment, mission-squawker, mountain-boomer, mush-mouth, peent, pink-wink, pipe-down, quit, rattle-box, razoo, rippit, saw-gourds, shivaree, sizzler, snickup, snurr, speakeasy, spieler, through, tin-ear, tizzicky, tree-squeak, tuckahoe, uncle-dudley, weeper, whistling-billy, whoop-up, window-rattler, woodin-up, woodpecker, yip.

BIBLIOGRAPHY

Akerman, J. Y. *A Glossary of Provincial Words and Phrases in use in Wiltshire.* London, 1842.

Angelicus, D. *The Vulgar Tongue, comprising two glossaries of slang, cant and flash words and phrases, principally used in London at the present day.* London, 1857.

Angus, J. S. *A Glossary of the Shetland Dialect.* Paisley, 1914.

Atkinson, J. C. *A Glossary of the Cleveland Dialect.* London, 1868.

Badcock, J. *Sportman's slang; a new dictionary.* London, 1825.

Bailey, N. and Axon, W. E. *English Dialect Words of the Eighteenth Century.* London. 1883.

Baker, P. *Fantabulosa: a dictionary of Polari and gay slang.* London, 2002.

Baker, S. J. *New Zealand Slang. A dictionary of colloquialisms.* Christchurch, 1941.

Baker, S. J. *The Drum. Australian character and slang.* Sydney, 1959.

Baker, S. J. *The Australian language.* Sydney, 1966.

Barnes, W. *A Glossary of the Dorset Dialect.* London, 1886.

Barrère, A. and Leland, C. G. *A Dictionary of Slang, Jargon and Cant.* London, 1897.

Bath, C. S. and Crofton, H. T. *The Dialect of the English Gypsies.* London, 1875.

Body, G. *The railway language: a collection of railway terms and expressions.* Bristol, 1972.

Bowen, F. C. *Sea Slang. A dictionary of the old-timers' expressions and epithets, etc.* London, 1929.

Brewer, E. C. *Sound and its Phenomena.* London, 1854.

Britten, J. and Holland, R. *A Dictionary of English Plant-names.* London, 1886.

Cassidy, F. G. *Jamaica talk: Three hundred years of the English language in Jamaica.* Kingston, 1982.

Caulfield, J. *Blackguardiana.* London, 1793.

Cole, R. E. G. *A Glossary of Words used in South-west Lincolnshire, Wapentake of Graffoe.* London, 1886.

Cooper, W. D. *A Glossary of the Provincialisms in use in the County of Sussex.* Brighton, 1836.

Cope, W. H. *A Glossary of Hampshire Words and Phrases.* London, 1883.

Courtney, M. A. and Couch, T. Q. *Glossary of Words in use in Cornwall.* London, 1880.

Dartnell, G. E. and Goddard, E. H. *A Glossary of Words used in the County of Wiltshire.* London, 1893.

Davidson, T. (ed.) *Chambers's Twentieth Century Dictionary of the English Language.* London and Edinburgh, 1908.

Dickinson, W. *A Glossary of the Words and Phrases of Cumberland.* Whitehaven, 1859.

Dinsdale, F. T. *A Glossary of Provincial Words used in the County of Durham.* London, 1849.

Ditchfield, P. H. *Old English Sports, Pastimes and Customs.* London, 1891.

Easther, A. *A Glossary of the Dialect of Almondbury and Huddersfield.* London, 1883.

Engel, C. *Musical instruments.* London, 1908.

Farmer, J. S. and Henley, W. E. *A dictionary of slang and colloquial English.* London, 1905.

Ferguson, R. *The Dialect of Cumberland.* London, 1873.

Forby, R. *Vocabulary of East Anglia: an attempt to record the vulgar tongue of the counties Norfolk and Suffolk.* 1830.

Franklyn, J. *A Dictionary of Rhyming Slang*. London, 1960.

Fraser, E. and Gibbons, J. *Soldier and sailor words and phrases*. London, 1925.

Gepp. E. *An Essex Dialect Dictionary*. London, 1923.

Gosse, P. H. *The Birds of Jamaica*. London, 1847.

Gower, G. W. *A glossary of Surrey words*. London, 1893.

Granville, W. *Sea Slang of the Twentieth Century*. London, 1949.

Grose, F. *Dictionary of the Vulgar Tongue*. London, 1811.

Grose, F. *A glossary of local and provincial words used in England*. London, 1839.

Halliwell-Phillips, J. O. *A Dictionary of archaic and provincial words, obsolete phrases, proverbs and ancient customs from the fourteenth century*. London, 1855.

Hendrickson, R. *Encyclopedia of Word and Phrase Origins*. London, 1987.

Henke, J. T. *Gutter life and language in the early 'street' literature of England*. Connecticut, 1988.

Heslop, R. O. *Northumberland Words*. London, 1894.

Hipkins, A. J. *Musical instruments: historic, rare and unique*. Edinburgh, 1888.

Holland, R. *A Glossary of Words used in the County of Chester*. London, 1886.

Hotten, J. C. *The Slang Dictionary, etc*. London, 1872.

Hunt, J. L. and Pringle, A. G. *Service slang: a first selection*. 1943.

Hunt, T. *Plant names of medieval England*. 1989.

Huntley, R. W. *A Glossary of the Cotswold (Gloucestershire) Dialect*. London, 1868.

Irwin, G. *American tramp and underworld slang*. London, 1931.

Jennings, J. *The Dialect of the West of England*. London, 1869.

Kendall, S. T. *Up the frog. The road to Cockney rhyming slang*. London, 1969.

Kirby, B. *Lakeland Words: A Collection of Dialect Words and Phrases*. Kendal, 1898.

Long, E. *The History of Jamaica*. London, 1774.

Long, W. H. *A Dictionary of the Isle of Wight Dialect, and of Provincialisms used in the Island.* London, 1886.

Lowsley, B. *A Glossary of Berkshire Words and Phrases.* London, 1888.

Marples, M. *Public school slang.* London, 1940.

Mayer, A. M. *Sound: a series of simple, entertaining, and inexpensive experiments in the phenomena of sound.* London, 1881.

Mayhew, A. L. *Concise dictionary of middle English from A.D. 1150 to 1580.* Oxford, 1888.

McKenna, F. *A glossary of railwaymen's talk.* Oxford, 1970.

Minard, B. *How to talk proper in Liverpool.* Liverpool, 1972.

Moore, A. W. *A Vocabulary of the Anglo-Manx Dialect.* London, 1924.

Nall, J. G. *Chapters on the East Anglian coast.* London, 1866.

Nance, R. M. *A Glossary of Cornish Sea-Words.* Marazion, 1963.

Nodal, J. H. and Milner, G. *A Glossary of the Lancashire Dialect.* London, 1875.

Northall, G. F. *A Warwickshire Word-book.* London, 1896.

Parish, W. D. & Master, J. *A Dictionary of the Kentish Dialect and provincialisms in use in the County of Kent.* London, 1887.

Parish, W. D. *A Dictionary of the Sussex Dialect and collection of provincialisms in use in the County of Sussex.* Lewes, 1875.

Partridge, E. *A dictionary of slang and unconventional English.* London, 1949.

Patterson, W. H. *A Glossary of Words in the Counties of Antrim and Down.* London, 1880.

Pease, A. E. *A Dictionary of the Dialect of the North Riding of Yorkshire.* Whitby, 1928.

Pegge, S. *Anecdotes of the English Language.* London, 1814.

Phillips, I. *Rhyming Slang: A concise dictionary.* London, 1932.

Robertson, J. D. *A Glossary of Dialect & Archaic Words used in the County of Gloucester.* London, 1890.

Senior, B. M. *Jamaica as it was, as it is, and as it may be.* London, 1835.

Sheppard, H. *Dictionary of railway slang.* Ilminster, 1967.

Smart, B. C. *The Dialect of the English Gypsies.* London, 1875.

Stevens-Cox, J. *An Ilchester word list and some folklore notes*. St Peter Port, 1974.

Stubbings, F. H. *Bedders, bulldogs and bedells: a Cambridge glossary*. Cambridge, 1995.

Swainson, C. *The folklore and provincial names of British birds*. London, 1886.

Ware, J. R. *Passing English of the Victorian Era*. London, 1909.

Webster, N. and Porter, N. *Webster's Revised Unabridged Dictionary*. Springfield, 1913.

Wentworth, H. *American Dialect Dictionary*. New York, 1944.

Weseen, M. H. *A dictionary of American slang*. Shanghai, 1946.

Wilbraham, R. and Leigh, E. *A Glossary of Words used in the Dialect of Cheshire*. London, 1877.

Wright, J. *The English Dialect Dictionary*. London, 1898.

Wright, T. *Dictionary of Obsolete and provincial English*. 1893.

Yaxley, D. *A researcher's glossary of words found in historical documents of East Anglia*. Dereham, 2003.

Yule, H. *Hobson-Jobson: being a glossary of Anglo-Indian colloquial words and phrases, and of kindred terms*. London, 1886.

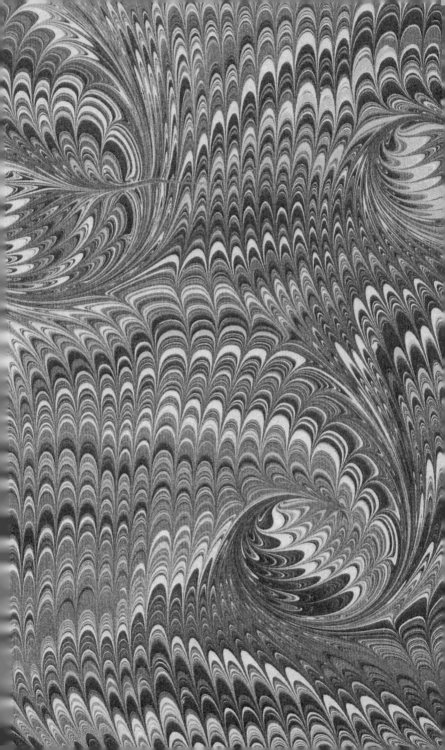

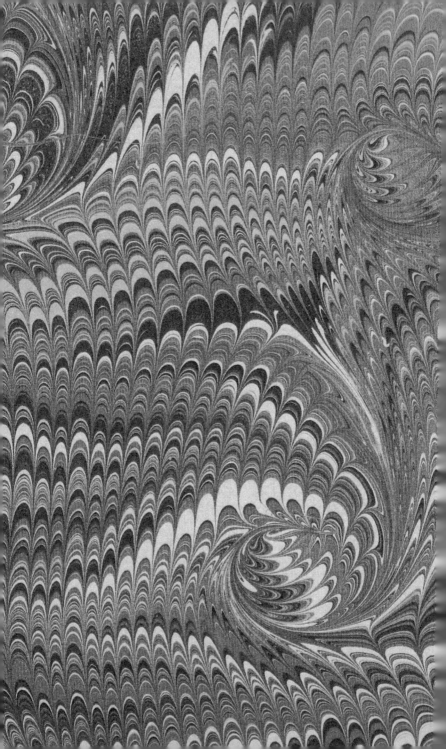